My Sum, "The Doctor"

Jonathan Singer, MD

PublishAmerica
Baltimore

First printing

ISBN: 1-59129-648-X
PUBLISHED BY PUBLISHAMERICA BOOK PUBLISHERS
www.publishamerica.com
Baltimore

Printed in the United States of America

Dedication

To my three class-C knothole baseball coaches. I thank Millard Mack for surrendering the 30", 30 oz. Adirondack bat at season's end despite my inability to achieve a high batting average. I thank Art Cole for telling my dad to go easy on me after I participated with my friends on a post-practice impromptu rock-breaking of elementary school windows. I thank John P., a vice-president of a major shoe company. I was the only kid on the team without baseball spikes, and he promised a pair and never delivered. At age 11, I learned the virtues of deliverance, trust and deceit.

Acknowledgements

I've long concluded the public image and private thoughts of who I am are the sum of interconnecting sequences. It seems a loosely-bound assemblage of plots on an imaginary graph have been formative from a time of my earliest recall through early adulthood. Some encounters have responsibly steered me toward credible propriety. Other situational circumstances have more influenced my untutored instincts toward frivolity.

My capacity for recall varies. Generally, I am unlikely to long remember meddlesome encounters that occur on a daily basis. In contrast, pleasurable adventures sustain attention far beyond the moment. Highly positive occurrences tend to be forever stored in my mental attic.

Four of my office mates, Linda Stanchina, Shirley Foreman, Lynn DeWine and Alaine White, took pleasure in translating my legal pad wanderings into text. I benefited from their valued contributions.

I am grateful to brother Barry Singer and cousin Leah Taylor, who provided encouraging commentary as they reviewed earlier drafts of the manuscript. I thank my wife, Ruth, for her earthy perspective and uniformly cautious honesty. I apologize for making her read poetry that had "moved on" since our earliest union.

I also apologize for those I know, who now or in the past held themselves partially responsible for my behaviors. With profound confession, I hope to have mended fences. I do not seek to further alienate my acquaintances. Although they are all portrayed by name, where commentary is potentially acrimonious, I have changed the name, not the attributes. I have blanketed all patients with pseudonyms. The patients have changed my life and comprehensions.

UNPRINCIPLED BEGINNINGS

CONCEPTION

Close your eyes and allow the rain to fall
Upon your lips and then
Extend your tongue and life begins.

THE COACH'S FAITH

For 11th grade English class we were required to write an autobiography. I plagiarized my older brother's. It had been three years since he had graduated from the same high school. I figured Mrs. Martin wouldn't remember his narrative.

Brother Barry had received an "A" on the manuscript. This was no surprise since he had sustained a straight "A" average while enrolled in all Advanced Placement subjects. Although brother's twelve-page, double-spaced, typed report detailed events that were quite dissimilar from mine, the theft was not deterred. I felt compelled to change only the portion that dealt with the most influential person in my life.

Whereas brother praised his 4th grade teacher for sparking his desire to explore sciences, I singled out Mr. Art Cole, my class-C knothole coach. It was Head Coach Cole and his two assistants during the 6th grade who fashioned my life.

Assistant John P., a young executive with a prominent shoe company, noted I was the only youngster without baseball shoes. He promised me a pair. They never came. I have ignored vacant promises from individuals without conviction since that season's end.

Because of Assistant Coach Millard Mack, I've admired the grace of those without obligation who give. Mr. Mack worked religiously on my efforts to hit a curve ball. I was then and remain now a weak batter with an excellent glove and a rifle arm. Millard failed to improve my swing, through no fault of his own. He spontaneously presented me our team's favored bat. The precious implement was painted black, lacquered and chipped only years later when I absentmindedly resorted to striking mud balls and rocks in the empty lot up the street.

Coach Cole viewed unseen potential of the human spirit. He told my dad I was a good kid. He said it with sufficient enthusiasm that I felt the juvenile record I had amassed was nullified by his conviction. When Mrs. Katona asked if I was involved with the window-breaking at North Avondale Elementary School, I answered without hesitation. Eugene, my best friend, born within six hours of my birth, denied his involvement. I temporarily cleansed my rotting soul with the truth. The Malman brothers instigated the rock-throwing after knothole practice. The rather innocent intent was not to destroy property, but to prove who had the most accurate throwing arm. The two panes I struck were already broken. Since I only hit damaged goods, I instantaneously felt absolved of wrongdoing. The delayed but unhesitant confession thus came easily.

The team and their parents were ultimately summoned to Coach Cole's house. Mom was the usual driver of the 1954 Plymouth, but on this occasion, Pop, in absolute silence, escorted me on foot in a manner I perceived as a death march. I longed for any communication and welcomed the justified scolding tone of the police officer who was in attendance at the meeting. Pop didn't speak to anyone until meeting's end when Mr. Cole interceded with his favorable assertion regarding my character. When we returned home, I didn't receive the obligatory and well-deserved belt across the buttocks.

Many others in succeeding years did not overlook the opportunity to drive sense into me through my back side.

THE COACH'S FOOT

Mr. Will Bass taught 11th grade co-ed health. We met for 40 minutes one day per week for half the school year. The curriculum was clearly defined in a text which Will neither emphasized nor discouraged. His only demand was that we not disrupt the silence of unofficial study hall. We were guaranteed an "A" if we followed his singular lesson delivered in early September. At the time, I was simply humored by his remark, which I recall with clarity. He had admonished us all, "Keep it in your pants and you'll stay out of trouble." At a time before sex education was commonplace, this assertion was as appropriate for our 1963 acne-covered faces as a more refined, contemporary plea for abstinence.

Will, the sage, was more accustomed to his role as a gym teacher. When the health semester metamorphosed to physical education, Will was again my preceptor. It was a late winter session of indoor fitness activities when I objected to the way Will measured Harold's length on a standing three jump. Harold Soloman and I hadn't even wagered the standard 56¢ sum that covered a full luncheon, including milk. I simply was too competitive to permit anyone to illegally out-perform me. Harold had fallen backwards, yet Will had ignored the trailing hands and placed the tape at Harold's feet.

I exclaimed, "You can't do that!"

Will retorted, "Don't you ever tell me what to do. Get your sorry ass out of here!" as he kicked me in the posterior.

Although the "F" in gym was less ominous than the "F" in 8th grade Latin, there were greater repercussions.

The State of Ohio required 3.5 credits of physical education for graduation from high school. Physical education was not offered as a summer school course. I had to make up the half credit senior year. I attended gym third bell, showered for senior English, and returned to gym fifth bell period. The first day of class we were assigned lockers and told to study the remainder of the hour. Bored, I took Rick Linsey's wager, betting that I could crawl through the basket rim 10' above the floor. I had one leg over the rim partially entangled in the net when the bell rang. I aborted the attempted self-basket just as the teacher, Whitey Ford, yelled, "Singer, get down!" After completing English class, I returned to the gym to be greeted by Whitey's paddle. I followed his instruction and removed my wallet and kerchief, then bent over. Despite one less finger on his right hand, Whitey's stroke was strong. The sting was delayed and I straightened up, begging for mercy.

The second strike was with equal intensity. Michael Lichtenstein, a visually-impaired classmate, moments later confided, "I couldn't see it Singer, but it sounded terrible."

SUBSTITUTES

Besides Whitey, Mr. Bill Lundsford, Mr. Biff Bailey and a substitute teacher in junior high whose name I never caught took turns with 8-12" wooden implements on my back side. The sub took it upon himself to straighten out Jerry Malman and I for hailing spit balls (discreetly, in my estimate) wide of his blackboard instruction.

MOTHERING

The sky is entwined with shades of pink and blue;
Of conflicting shapes and contrasting hues.
A feeling of softness over tree tops effuses,
Carrying the song of silence, expressing togetherness.
A blanket of darkness unrolls below the widest branches;
The night has begun in all its splendor.
In the hours to follow, unmoved were the stars
Still visible faintly through the clearing mist
Which rose near six to announce the morn.
Three drops of rain, no more
Caressed the family of black-eyed Susan
Yet a rainbow was cast in the storm
As the opossum emerged from the clearing
With the slumbering burden she was bearing.

Like mothers, substitutes were supposed to be treated with reverence. They came on a mission to fulfill the obligation of a full-time educator who was temporarily ill. We were repeatedly instructed to exhibit our best behavior with substitute teachers. As Walnut Hills High School students, we were to show these temporaries why our school, which attracted college-bound youth from all reaches of Cincinnati, was heads above the rest. As a rule, we were only slightly discourteous, particularly to the subs who filled in with regularity.

Mr. Fish, a diminutive, balding, bespeckeled, first-generation American, middle-aged bachelor delighted himself with math quizzes. It didn't matter which class he subbed for, he systematically besieged the inhabitants of the aisles for square roots and other mathematical abstractions. He was too weird to spoof.

We rarely stepped out of line for Skeejumps. She was an attractive, silver-haired woman with enormous breasts that had unsuccessfully battled gravity with the passage of time. Because she could execute a glance that could kill, the majority remained in line during her tutelage. Only Allen Kemper transgressed one afternoon. He received Skeejump's approval to visit the bathroom and rather than relieving himself, he detonated a toilet with several cherry bombs. Skeejumps was not forgiving, and Kemper became the school's official blackboard cleaner.

A punishment was more swift and just for Kemper when he and two colleagues cheated on a physics test. Three members of the social club, the D.B.s, turned in identical answers on a written exam. Unbeknownst to the class, Mr. Thompson distributed two different tests in alternating rows. When Kemper turned inappropriate answers for the test administered to his row, he was nailed. Thompson retained Kemper after class the following day, confronted Kemper then summarily punched him in the face. Kemper, a starting tackle, intuitively reciprocated and yielded only when Thompson took a knee to Kemper's groin. Thompson toted a black eye for awhile, but Kemper found lasting respect for physics.

The struggle I had with physics paled in comparison to ancient and medieval history.

THE A&M THAT WASN'T TEXAS

I took the selective in ancient and medieval history senior year. I had Barry's outlines that served as personalized Cliff's notes. For me, the outlines supplanted the text. Years earlier I had refined the art of creating miniature cheat sheets on a 6x1" scroll of paper, using a fine-tipped pen. I could easily commit several hundred years of A & M history on a compressed scroll that at times of test-taking either fit in the palm of my left hand or disappeared beneath my left thigh. With these crutches, I passed the course, but like my classmates I was preoccupied with distant thoughts in the classroom. I often spent the majority of the class time contemplating how to enter the school's bus at day's end without paying bus fare.

THE EPITAPH

Similar, with stubby nose and wanned skin,
Two specimen of equal rank exist.
Their mother's womb created he and him
And gave them common characteristics.
As the children grew from their foundations,
Their attitudes were from the same beliefs.
But like the death of half a branch, the actions
Of this bud debased the fruit. Released
With faith were all supernal character
Which changed the child to a supine adult.
This indifference to his needs deterred
A prolific life. Death was the result.
So long as brothers germinate, their hours
Of vitality will yield a different flow'r.

Few of my colleagues sensed the instructional relevance of these Old World events. Several rows about me, the kids whose last names began in S through Z seated at the far right-hand corner of the class maintained more attention toward the janitor. A slovenly gentleman, he pushed a cart to hallways end between 2:40 and 2:55 PM daily. We each contributed a dime and predicted the exact time he would pass our doorway. When the majority of classmates' eyes were half closed, our mutual pool was wide-eyed in anticipation.

Perhaps the excitement was too much one day when T.D. Spellman interrupted class with an agonizing sound and dropped to her knees, distributing a very small puddle of vomitus. The plastic mold, drawn from her purse and strategically placed at my feet, looked real, complete with identifiable chunks of what would have easily passed for our cafeteria's mystery meat. The substitute teacher scolded us for giggling.

"Oh my, the girl is sick. This is nothing to laugh about. Please go see the school nurse!"

With only a glint of accomplishment in her eyes, the barest perception of a smile (or was it a muscular contraction from nausea that drew back her lips, revealing beautifully over crowded lateral incisors?), she disappeared mid-class.

At 2:52 PM, the rumble of the janitor's cart was audible. Paul Simon, affectionately known as "Si," had at least $2 riding on the janitor's passage at 2:53 PM. Si prayed out loud for the official wall clock to tick. The murmurs of our click intensified. T.D. Spellman, complete with a janitor's cap reversed and only partially obscuring dependent braids, paraded by, escorting the broom cart, complete with cleaning apparatus. I literally fell out of my chair. At class's end, Si, who needed the gas money badly, interpreted the historical incident to his favor, and the mutual pool awarded him the daily pot.

THE LINE

In the early '60s, Si was 1/6th of a band. They chose the name "Them" about one year before the English band "Them" hit popularity charts with several 45's. The "Them" I hung around with made a record through a local recording studio that gave birth to James Brown. The musical accomplishment of Si's group barely made it out of the womb. The works of Eugene, Stan, Dana, George, Mary Ellen, and Si were known to the Mug Club, an establishment that hosted 3.2% beer-imbibing 18-year-olds and the Starlight Bar, a dive on the outreaches of civilization west of Cincinnati that awoke on alternate weekends when it invited unknowns to sit in for jam sessions.

With the exception of "The Bird's The Word," Si could not complete a vocalization without error. But oh, how he could play the guitar. The group's collective talents eventually won them victories at regional challenges of the bands and consistent bookings at all high school dances around Cincinnati. Until midwinter one year I attended with regularity most of their engagements, and we enjoyed each other's company. One Friday evening after a second pitcher of beer, I sensed an urgency to urinate. For some reason, I decided I couldn't make it up the flight of stairs at the Mug Club's only available men's room. I walked to the far corner of the cement dance floor, and while hidden from view by the speakers, I took a healthy leak against the wall. When I realized the stream took a dependent path toward the drain in the center of the dance floor, I became conscious of the embarrassment I caused. I left, placed a note of apology on the windshield of Si's car, and terminated my role as a groupie.

That transgression did little to ruin our relationship. When the band was idle, we rode around town together in either the decade-old Plymouth I inherited or Si's Black Beauty, the '57 Plymouth with a rebuilt '56 engine. The later replacement was necessitated because the car couldn't navigate the hills out of second gear on the way to school, and poorly transported his musical instruments on a flat stretch of road in drive. Although we burned a lot of gasoline in our immediate area, we invested significant time in three high-density Catholic neighborhoods. We were searching for girls from Regina, Marion, Mother of Mercy or our Lady of Angels high schools. We attended their post-athletic event dances or community-sponsored social gatherings. We believed that these young ladies, segregated in parochial high schools, were eager to socialize with us.

Our record for the least number of high school pick-ups during a two-year time frame remains intact three decades later. We never induced one female adventurer into our cars with the much- practiced line, "You've got 30 seconds to get your ass in this car!" If someone had responded positively to our invitation, I'm sure we would have been challenged beyond our capabilities.

A JOURNEY FROM WINTER QUARTERS

Proficient search among Autumn leaves
Permitted a sheltered retreat.
Supportive were fruits of the earth;
Met all the standards of quality.
But proportions were lacking of sundries
So Winter folk arose from sleep
To leave their tracks for others to seek.
Through heights of endless sea
On land, all habited in white
The crusaders crossed the winterbourne
Engrossed with feelings of omnipotence,
Reluctant to recede.

FEMALE PERSUASION

Long before high school I was awestruck by women. In the 5th grade, the first two of the species gained my attention. Betty Rappaport and Chi Chi Aliopolis were unique. They were the only ones in our elementary school who could both climb a 20' pole and run a 50-yard dash faster than me. My fascination with Betty was short-lived. Her too-distant personality neutralized her athletic prowess. On the other hand, Chi Chi's friendliness was and remains overpowering. She welcomed my visitation to her home after school and on weekends. With her younger sisters, we played endless games of hide and seek. We joined their neighbors in pick-up games with any type of ball.

In the summer before 6th grade, Chi Chi's father was transferred to Washington, D.C. I never saw her again, and the impact of her loss has been permanent.

DEPARTURE

A hazy blue sky with fluffs of clouds

Surround the trees, and without a sound
The wind induces leaves aground.
They depart from where they experienced life;
Uncoupled from their source of joy,
The distance to the earth a short sojourn
Brightly colored yet never to return.
The duration of their existence unperceived
Dreaming hopefully to once again unite.

In retrospect, the depths of my feelings for Inez Fine and Nancy Stillpass were more superficial. At the time, you could not have convinced me. They possessed breasts. They were both enrolled in a twelve-week dance class intended to serve the dual purposes of exposure to modern dance and boy/girl etiquette. Nancy humored me with weekly partnership during cha cha. I favored her kiss during spin-the-bottle games at instructional breaks. I sought extra-curricular contact, but our relationship ended. Inez possessed equal beauty, a mischievous sense of humor and braces that somehow inhibited close contact with her mouth. I could not achieve greater attention from Inez despite my wish fulfilling gift to her of a 100-count box of Double Bubble gum on Valentine's Day. She favored Bill Katz and Steve Royale, both of whom who had reached puberty before me. Revenge came. Bill balded quite early and Steve's early growth spurt left him shorter than the rest of us when our testosterone kicked in during the 7th grade.

It's easy to believe that hormones caused me to treat Sharon Okrent so badly. However, my first official date in the 8th grade with Sharon was simply the result of my character flaw. Sharon, nick-named "Squirrel" by Mr. Bailey, was academically gifted. She was assigned to sit in the row forward and to the left of me in Latin class. I proposed she permit me to cheat off her during a crucial examination in exchange for a dance date. Sharon accepted and our misguided bond extended for an additional year without a *quid pro quo* relationship.

MORE LOST LOVE

Whereas I can recall none of Chi Chi's physical features, portions of Laura's body that I viewed are cast in my memory bank. For example, I can still see an indentation from a scratched chicken pox scab resting on her central forehead. Laura's physical appearance earned her the nickname "Popeye." She had an athletic, sinewy lower body and Skeejump's soft upper body, but without the demonstrable downward slope. From a distance, I observed her cheerlead and dance in school plays. I engaged her infrequently in conversation through my friendship with her older brother.

The summer I graduated high school, I took a job northwest of Indianapolis, 140 miles from home. For ten weeks I was head of a grounds crew at a camp. For the first eight weeks of the summer Laura had signed up as a babysitter for the administrative staff's kids. Neither of us earned significant dollars but we escaped the watchful eye of our parents and gained some sense of freedom. Like all employees of the camp, we were free to roam the acreage of the camp grounds when off duty. Occasionally, we would violate boundaries traveling to Beeler's and Rock Island properties, an adjacent farmer and oil refinery respectively.

SWINGING BRIDGE

**Inconstant breezes shake softened planks
That overlay the metal frame
Of yonder swinging bridge.
Gloriously she spans to Rock Island's banks
Peaking sharply at both water edges
But slackened, pendulous in between.
Beeler's hook can rest at depth
To avert the rotted wood and pungent weeds
That float in stagnant pockets at the periphery.
Far from nondescript, she transcends man-made beauty.**

Laura and I often took walks and established territories under various shade trees to talk. Within a month, she visited while I stripped the Recreation Hall floor. When I was free, I helped her babysit. At night, we held each other and talked of aspirations. I knew her as an exploratory person, not as a silhouette. She was a sensitive spirit who resisted authority and resented prejudice.

IN THE AMPHITHEATRE

We heard not the sound of thunder
When the oranges changed to gray.
The yellow was diverted;
Pastels had passed away.
Our whispers added to the silence
Our shadow to the darkness.
We hardly felt the rain.

One Friday night Laura and a member of the secretarial pool were granted an evening pass. I'm unsure of her companion, but Laura told me she had intercourse with several members of the band they picked up in an adjacent town. The mental picture was disturbing. I had no right to judge her actions. My acceptance permitted us to grow closer before she returned home. Letters and poems which we exchanged were insufficient contact.

In August of that year, the dad of one of my maintenance crew members, Brad Smoltz, was jailed back home. Donnie Rizzover's dad was hospitalized. As the maintenance crew director, I petitioned the camp director to borrow the camp station wagon for a Saturday afternoon. We arose before dawn, completed our maintenance chores. Under the guise of going to downtown Indianapolis for a movie and dinner, we drove to Cincinnati at 110 mph down Interstate 74. With such a sustained overdrive, the engine overheated 30 miles outside of Cincinnati, setting us back an hour or so and emptying us of cash. However, we all spent time with someone we loved before returning at nightfall to Indianapolis tardy but fulfilled. Two weeks later, we presented the auto repair bill to the camp director. We tore off the header of the bill that bore the address of Harrison, Ohio.

By the time Smoltz was on his way to Kenyon College and I enrolled at University of Cincinnati, Laura returned to her senior year at Walnut Hills. We lost the intimacy of our confinement. I had commissioned Selma Freck, an artist friend of my parents, to paint a seashore scene representing Laura's untamed spirit. On her 16th birthday, the first day of autumn, I presented her the frameless artwork. Shortly thereafter she retreated to her own world. To this day, my thoughts each September 21st gravitate to what ifs.

MY CONSTANT DREAM

The blankets need not cover your face
For all that is feared at night
Will pass to some other place.
There is no need to feign slumber;
The covers will rise and fall naturally.
My hand will soothe your body,
My breath caress the air you breathe.
I will be the guardian of your soul.
Sleep child and dream
Of the children that you will bear
When we are married.
I alone will have the nightmare of rejection.

MISSED FEMININE SIGNALS

I should have long recognized that gifts were useless methods of attraction. When not playing stick ball on the graveled street of my elementary years, I'd hang out with twin sisters who occupied the house Pop built. We had moved across the street to a larger house in an effort to accommodate Grandpa Rukin, whose health was in rapid decline. I offered the McKenna sisters a new ball and jacks. They rebuffed my advance.

At 16, I visited brother who was in grad school at Berkeley. He lent me his ID for boarding a tour bus. We arrived in Reno, Nevada at 2 AM in time to see the last show at a casino. After, I cashed in my $10 chip voucher and added $20 hard-earned but soon-to-be-disposable dollars. The chips disappeared long before the scheduled 7 AM bus return trip. Before dawn, I wandered to the lake. On retracing steps, I spotted a woman across the street standing on a corner. I figured she was a lady of the evening. I contemplated the pros and cons of making her an offer with my remaining cash. I looked both ways and stopped midway across the street. I yielded to an approaching high school bus that slowed, stopped, departed and left me by myself. That misplaced advance would surely have been rebuffed.

At the end of an evening, by which time I was convinced she was the most beautiful girl I had ever seen, I introduced myself to the young lady across the wedding rehearsal dinner table. Weeks later, after recurrent thoughts of her appearance, I contacted the mother of the bride, who supplied the name and ultimately the address of Dawn, a Chicago inhabitant. I wrote. She returned comments and we exchanged letters for a season. When she felt comfortable after several months into her freshman year at Indiana University, I traveled to Bloomington. I took her Saturday morning to Brown County State Park and the adjacent town, Nashville, Indiana. I returned her to campus at 5 PM and asked her out for Sunday morning brunch. I figured she needed a respite from me for Saturday evening. She erroneously sensed my lack of a Saturday evening pursuit of her company as disinterest.

A TRIP

The shadowed form of animals
Take shape, then disappear.
Elephants with many trunks
Grow horns, becoming deers.
Toadstools reach tremendous heights
Block sunshine meant for leaves
Of green, that fall, turn brown

Beneath the surface of the sea.
Single toothed Jack-o-lantern
With dimpled smile it can not hide
Watches witch, who hunches at her wheel
Transforming natural earthen clay
Through magic forces unreal
For the purpose of display.
When sent to bed without a meal,
Life's distorted by your tears.

NOT ALL MISFORTUNE

There were many misadventures in my youth that did not involve women. The first within memory was when a home-to-be owner made a Sunday visitation at his construction site. He found me with my pants at my ankles. I was able to leave my deposit in his yet-unconnected commode, raise my drawers and scramble between his legs. Brother, in exploration of the truly unfinished basement, conspired to deny our trespass. We successfully convinced a police officer of our innocence, but I suspect Pop's suspicions were aroused.

Father was remarkably understanding when I gave the finger to the "Brothers" and the "Sisters." They were the widowed and spinster siblings two doors away who stayed behind their persistently closed Venetian blinds and spied on the neighborhood. When they drove their ancient, four-door sedan at a Sunday go-to-meeting speed through our baseball game on the street, I gave them the universal signal. They apparently weren't pleased. In a half-hour or so I heard Pop's frantic apology to someone's confrontational call. Pop's demeanor abruptly changed when I assume the caller suggested a specific punishment or indicated I needed an improved upbringing. I only heard Pop tell them something rude as he slammed the phone. Father asked that I be more tolerant than he.

I did receive greater punishment when one of the Brothers aborted my attempt at stuffing a stray cat down a sewer opening, tangential to one of their peep holes.

ROAD TO RECOVERY

Whether successful or not with the cat killing, at many points before maturity I should have been incarcerated, even if it was only for the shoplifting. The penalty for shoplifting would have been light were it not for the repetitive nature of the offense. I practiced stealth most frequently at Clyde's Apothecary. The pickings were good, but Clyde kept the best candy enshrouded in classic candy cases. Ron's was an easier target for two reasons. One, the cashier counter attendant's view of the candy rack was blinded by shelving; and two, the owner, Ron was blind. Only when wife Angie was at the post did you need to be vigilant. In the 8th grade, when I did get caught with five pieces of fingered Double Bubble and was interrogated, I indicated they had caught Paul Simon. I provided Si's address and telephone number on demand. On the bicycle flight on the way home, I diverted from a straight path. I had discussions with God. We settled on a more rigorous path toward honesty.

PLACENTATION

Poppies seek at birth
The sea-born breeze
For they were implanted
Within the restless
Bound of the ocean spray
Entangled in the erosive
Vomitus of foreign origin.
Brown-green wreaths washed
Naked by salt and rock
Are left to rot upon the sands
To decay and nurture life.

LAST TRANSGRESSION

In my freshman year at the University of Cincinnati, I froze the moment a math exam was distributed. I couldn't begin any of the first three problems. In a whispered voice, I asked the person next to me which equation to apply. The immediate panic resolved. The more disturbing thought centered on my violation of the covenant I had observed for three years.

If you exclude the perusal of old examinations that were housed in multiple fraternity house libraries, I was otherwise honest in college. Year after year, several of Dr. Relehan's multiple choice chemistry questions would be repeated. You could count on Dr. Romano to resurrect a microbiology exam question, particularly essays from the preceding decade. There were guys like Larry Rinsky that could effortlessly answer any style of question correctly.

RINSKY

Larry Rinsky, to my knowledge, was like me, the middle child of a not particularly affluent family. He graduated from Woodward High School, a competitor with Walnut Hills. Rinsky obtained a 4.0 grade point average, less a singular "B" in physical education. He was the most prominent student with me at the University of Cincinnati. In the three years that we shared classroom hours, he was admired for his appearance (tall, tanned, terribly handsome with a Kennedyish smile) and demeanor (controlled, confident, and colossally successful). Above all else, everyone looked up to Rinsky for his consistent acquisition of the highest grade among us, irrespective of the class size or orientation. I, on the other hand, traditionally achieved the lowest possible numerical grade that constituted an "A" based on the Rinsky curve. I became known as the "poor man's Rinsky" and kept the title in my senior year although Rinsky had moved on to the University of Cincinnati College of Medicine as an early entrant. In order to raise to the level of poor man's Rinsky, I needed to review old examination questions whenever available.

CHURCHILL, A ROSE

Churchill McKinney, did not to my knowledge, have a conversion to honesty. She was always open, forthright and accepting from the minute we crossed paths in junior high. She would score only a few points below me in college while purposely avoiding contact with pilfered exams. She was intent, like the rest of us pre-med majors, on being a physician. She changed her mind senior year of college, withdrew her application and pursued successfully a Ph.D. in microbiology.

CHURCHILL, A ROSE

She cherished her friendship with mother earth;
Oftentimes spoke words of kindness
In secluded adventure within the woods.
Timeless were her rays of sun
However timeworn were her paths.
No life was plagued with emptiness,
Nor death without its reason.
Beneath a tender sapling she played
And viewed the easting light,
Unspotted by the bounds of age.
She had a fragrance that could be tasted,
A sweetness that could be heard.

Without Churchill, I would not have made it into medical school. I would not even have survived the undergraduate microbiology laboratory course. As my partner, she led me through a torture called tube dilutions. The process permitted you to calculate the growth rate of a quantum of bacteria. To obtain an answer, you needed a facility with math. I lacked the requisite knowledge which should have been acquired in the 5th grade. However, Ms. Downing was charged with teaching new math that year in our experimental elementary school class. I couldn't grasp the concepts she offered. She often grasped my neck. The result has been a life-long deficit with numbers.

Churchill, a gentile, crossed high school religious boundaries and dated Jews. She also was comfortable with group outings. Many of my male friends cherished her company. In college, she acquired a steady boyfriend in freshman year. They fought sporadically and eventually were married. They were at a point of separation at Churchill's sorority's Christmas formal. She asked me to fill in. I bought her a corsage of miniature roses, and she has been the only woman in my life who's received this symbol of affection.

By knowing Churchill, I knew Sandy Goyett and Barb Shaup. Sandy was a semi-natural blond attracted to rich men with a pension for snow skiing. I was without affluence, but I did inherit my father's khaki-colored, double-breasted, circa 1940 raincoat which I wore in microbiology lab in lieu of a mandatory white lab coat. The apparel impressed Sandy, but perhaps in the wrong way. Adjacent to Sandy in the lab was Ruth, my eventual soul mate who I married six years later. Ruth recalls some nut wore a raincoat in micro lab but thankfully failed to make the association three years later when we met again, for the first time.

Barb Shaup was segregated alphabetically by the University of Cincinnati into my English class. She recognized me as Churchill's friend. Barb was a small Indiana farming community product with country innocence, sparkling blue eyes and a zest for aiding others. I was never brave enough to ask Barb out. As a result of a late autumn day when our professor forgot to show for class, I almost had the courage. After all of the classmates left, Barb and I spent the hour discussing the poetry assignment. Shakespeare held your attention, but I thought our chemistry was a potential couplet. Shortly thereafter, at the Christmas formal with Churchill, I witnessed my first and only "candle passing ceremony." During the event, Barb blew out the flame on the third pass around the circled sorority sisters, signaling the announcement of her engagement. More than one flame expired that evening.

DECEMBER FLOWERAGE

Let me leave the sheltered beneath
And rise above the earth to challenge the light.
Just once I want to catch the wind
And stare into the flawless heaven.
No common thoughts reside within;
No lesser goals that can be kindled
On wayward paths or deceitful venture.
Self-born wisdom shall I bear
And cure the aged of their ills.
Deny me not, oh Hallowed Lord!
Rescind the laws of Ancient lore,
And permit my birth unseasoned be.

THE OTHER FLAME

A flame resided in many of my college classmates. The flicker was for medical school. In some cases, like Tommy Kreindler, the passing was seemingly inherited. All three Kreindler kids were enrolled into their dad's allergy practice like the Wallendas at an early age. The transition from the kids' unofficial internship into medial school held less of a thrill than a high wire act. For the rest of my friends, entrance to med school was a long-held dream.

In order for all of us to get there, we had to take among others, organic chemistry and physics. Organic was unintelligible to all but the chemistry majors. No matter how attentive you were in class, the speed of your note taking, or the thoroughness of your underlined reading assignments, very little sunk in. Although I preferred solitary study, I needed to bounce my organic thoughts off Harold Soloman and Abe Ross. In order to accommodate our varying schedules, I sponsored a 5:30 AM meeting at my place. Harold was dropped off by his date. The three of us synthesized compounds on paper together with Harold's eyes half-closed.

Abe was of a small group of "weak sisters," according to our college

German professor. Despite Abe's Polish ancestry and a household language of Yiddish, Abe earned "Cs" and "Ds" in German and English. All other grades were "A's" as he rivaled Rinsky in sciences. Abe had taken Dr. Joiner's calculus-based physics class. Abe mastered both organic chemistry and physics concurrently, whereas other premedical students suffered. By midterm, many premeds switched college majors. I strategically delayed physics until senior year. I was a solid "B" student the first two semesters and pulled Abe with me into Dr. Joiner's office third semester to beg for a marginally deserved "B." The plan worked.

In junior year, we all took the Medical Collegiate Aptitude Test (M.C.A.T.), a standardized eight-hour examination marathon. The first half of the standardized test measures comprehension of the written word and your capacity to spontaneously write a composition from a supplied thesis statement. The second half of the test asks you to apply your concrete knowledge of biologic science and physical sciences. I performed less well than the national average, in part because I had not yet taken physics.

I had taken a standardized test in the 6th grade in order to gain entrance into prestigious Walnut Hills High School. Elementary students from Cincinnati's Public School's system were invited to Walnut Hills only if they passed at least three of four test components. I passed exactly 75% of the test. My one quarter failure resulted from spending one-third of the allowable minutes contemplating the correct response from among four offerings on a single question. I didn't know the answer then and I don't know the answer now. It has haunted me to not understand, "Why is there snow on the top of a mountain when the peak is closer to the sun?"

Facing the physics section of the M.C.A.T. was reminiscent of the Walnut Hills entrance test, only worse. To this day, I repeatedly have nightmares. Although there is variation, the general theme is as follows. A test is being distributed. Others apply their number two pencils, but I fail to comprehend the instruction or cannot respond to any of the questions raised. In a panic, I awake. Typically, I tell myself this is a dream but concentrate to revive the non-existent question and answer it before returning to sleep.

ANOTHER NIGHTMARE

Relative to many states, Ohio is blessed with an abundance of medical schools. Although there are cyclical trends and yearly variations, roughly 4,000 Ohioans each year take the M.C.A.T.s and send in applications to the state's medical schools. From this large applicant pool the average Ohio school selects up to 400 students to interview. From the 400 who interview, 125 are eventually accepted into each medical school. At the time of my application in 1967, there were eleven people seeking each available position throughout the Ohio schools. That prospect alone was intimidating, particularly with less than average M.C.A.T. scores. Abe had interviewed at the University of Cincinnati College of Medicine several weeks before I was invited. He said he could see through the back of his transcript held before his interviewer's eyes. The "Cs" and "Ds" had been circled. His mouth went dry.

Since odds were against you, pre-medical students then and now apply to over a dozen schools in and out of the state. In 1967, the fee was $35 per school, which was a not an insignificant expense when you were penniless. I applied only to U.C.'s College of Medicine, placing all eggs so to speak in one basket.

By interview eve I had responded repeatedly to my own face in the mirror. I had projected a majority of the questions and worked extra hard on facial expressions coupled with intonations that suggested spontaneity, confidence with humility. The microbiology professor who interviewed me was new to the Admission's Committee. He seemed more nervous than I. I lost confidence when he implied midway through the hour that I was unlikely to gain acceptance at U.C. He found my selectivity foolish and directed me to apply to ten schools that he named.

WINTER'S REJECTION

Fresh was the tremulant wind;
Dissonant, yet of poetic composition,
That caused the transformation

And allowed it to descend.
For months it was suppliant
And avowed The Reverence,
For it dearly wanted lodgement.
But for the enchanting water
The Autumn fragrance was now a reflection;
A sorrel and golden motif.
No longer did it flow or ripple,
And accepted not the leaf.

Two hours after arriving home, the microbiology professor called. He told me I need not apply to other schools. I went from the depth of depression to the height of elation. I don't know why he provided me this exceptional courtesy two months before an official acceptance letter. I suspect some supervisory committee member interceded to rectify the impression of certain rejection.

HUMBLED DURING MEDICAL SCHOOL

THE CONVOCATION

After the Dean and administrative staff welcomed us, a professor of psychiatry presented the first formal lecture to our assembled class. He indicated our education would resemble our predecessors'. We would receive instruction regarding the wonders of the human mind and body. On behalf of all of our professors, he assured us their intention was to have 100% of us graduate. Further, he said, "In my day, they told us to look to your left, look to your right. One of you won't make it until the end of four years. These days are gone. We will do everything in our power to have you receive a doctor of medicine degree."

FIRST TEST

Unfortunately, the first medical student drop-out occurred within six weeks. He committed suicide by drinking a concentrated acid solution. The brutal exit from school and life was a combination of factors. He had come from three ancestral lines of physicians. He was a music major at Oberlin College, yet entered medical school to appease his physician father and physician uncle. The morning of the last day of his life, we all took an open book written examination in biochemistry. We were instructed to choose 100 points worth of questions from 235 available points. We could use any notes and any textbook as a resource. We had 2 ½ hours to fill in a dozen 8 ½ x 11" forms. After surveying the entire test, I responded to the questions that appeared easiest. On that Friday morning I wrote furiously. When Professor Rudney announced "one hour to go," I had answered only 55 points. The remaining time I was panic-stricken and I knew (erroneously) I had failed when the papers were collected. I looked left and looked right. I needed a drink of alcohol, not acid.

A FOOLISH OUTLET

That evening I joined most of my freshman class at Tommy Kreindler's apartment. I took a full bottle of Jack Daniels and drank too much before driving home. I chauffeured two new acquaintances, dietary students, back to their college dorm. I don't remember the drive from that point on. I awoke with the car five feet forward of my standard parking place with the right front end of the car at the curb and the right rear, two feet into the street. There was vomitus all over my lap. I never repeated the stupidity of that moment.

I permanently gave up alcohol as a means of mental release. I reserved small volumes of hard liquor or wine for a more refined, infrequent social event. I enjoyed beer after cutting grass. Yard work became my favorite stress reliever. It has occasionally afforded unexpected contacts.

THREE CHILDREN MET ON SATURDAY

As I was tending the lawn today
A younger child by nine months it seemed
Wanted to know what I kept 'tween my teeth
So she whispered quite loud to her older sister
Whose ear it seemed was mildly tickled.
After a giggle and a shrug of a shoulder
She asked why I should chew grass.
I turned as if quite startled
And replied cause it tastes like it oughta.
I thought no more of the answer you see,
Till the younger stood with a grin
Complete with a green stem upon it.
I know your name, it's funny face.
How do you grow a beard?

(Came a voice from behind my knee)
Well, when you get to be sixteen or so
Hair on your face begins to grow
And if you don't cut it each day
A beard can grow this way.
My brother has a moustache, said she.
I asked how old would he be?
He is this many, her fingers told me.
My sister has one too,
A point I didn't pursue.
Two complications I have clarified.
The question remains as how to explain
One back yard full of weeds.

ANATOMY

Besides microbiology, the other major courses in the first semester were Gross Anatomy and Microscopic Anatomy. In Microanatomy laboratory, we found the microscope stations arranged alphabetically. In microanatomy lecture, there was open seating. I arbitrarily picked the left of aisle seat in the front row. After one sleepless night, the monotony of the professor drew my eyes closed. I don't know how long I was out. I startled to a state of awareness. The classroom burst into laughter. My first thought was that they were laughing at me, but it was only a well-delivered punch line and a coincident neck snap.

After lunch, three days per week we dissected a body. On the first day you were afraid of your reaction to 50 deceased, phenol-impregnated individuals stacked in parallel on raised aluminum tables. There was relative silence as we all paraded to our assigned Gross Anatomy table. The bodies were prone since we began with the back musculature. It wasn't until the second semester when we moved to head and neck that we removed the burlap bag that masked the face of the person who generously donated their body for our education. We were never told the person's real name. My anatomy partners, Hugh Hu, Harold Soloman, Abe Ross, and I named our gentleman Frank.

Diagonally across from us was Warren Marcawski, who was height-challenged. On a late winter afternoon we entered the skulls of our cadavers. Warren was standing on the table wielding his buzz saw while straddling his cadaver. The enthusiasm Warren exhibited for his cadaver's brain was well suited. He became one of two neurosurgeons in our graduating class.

CHOOSING A SPECIALTY

During college, I would occasionally ride in Warren's Barracuda. Interspersed with tire screeching, Warren would talk of his father's internal medicine practice. After straight "Cs" for two years, during which time Warren gave greater effort for the University of Cincinnati wrestling team, he spoke of pursuing medicine. Warren received straight "A's" for the last two years of college and performed above the mean on the M.C.A.T.s. Whereas Abe and I were accepted to medical school by Thanksgiving, Warren was interviewed late and placed on a wait list. Only when an accepted candidate committed to another medical school in May or June was Warren then accepted to U.C. The uphill fight for acceptance hardened Warren's fierce competitive state, and he separated from the rest of us. Becoming a neurosurgeon was natural for a distant, short-statured muscle man, intermittently melancholic with a persistent chip on his shoulder.

Hugh Chung-Tai Hu was the oldest child of three who immigrated to the U.S. at a young age. Hugh had relatives in America but became the self-reliant protector of his younger siblings. He believed in the traditions of his ancestors. During his senior year he traveled to Taiwan to find his bride. Upon returning, he entered general practice training in order to take care of the entire needs of families he would encounter.

Abe was drawn to anesthesiology. He saw that the practice required a high degree of understanding for a limited number of circumstances. He envied the anesthesiologists' technical capabilities and perceived the leadership in the operating room emanated from the anesthesiologist, not the surgeon. Abe, Stuart Cutler and I were assigned our third year of medical school as a team to a community hospital for a four week obstetrical (OB) and gynecological (Gyn) experience. Abe was fascinated with one anesthesiologist who successfully passed the gas, monitored the patient's progress, read the financial page of the *Wall Street Journal* and formulated a billing statement in the course of the patient's hysterectomy.

Upon entering medical school, I projected being a practitioner of obstetrics and gynecology. I knew no one who practiced this specialty. I never had an opportunity of shadowing any physician. In my mind, the obstetrical portion of the OB-Gyn field would permit me to bring new life into the world. Stuart felt the same way. He also felt Gyn practice permitted you to care for all ages of women. A skilled OB-Gyn physician practiced psychiatry, surgery, and for complex cases, a sophisticated level of internal medicine. The field demanded intelligence, stamina and sensitivity. By month's end, it was apparent that Stuart chose to attend to the mothers' needs and I was drawn to the infants.

MY AWAKENINGS

For the first two years of medical school, patient contact was rare. An exception occurred every Friday. We gathered in a steeply pitched, circular theater for a course entitled "Introduction to Clinical Medicine" (I.C.M.). During I.C.M., a professor would typically introduce us to a patient who was chronically afflicted with a disease process. The professor would delineate the clinical manifestations of the disease. The patient would then detail how the disease state became apparent. The patient often shared how their life was impacted by the disease state. I found these experiences poignant and revealing. Disease leapt from the pages of our textbooks. When the patient's inhibitions did not block their speech, we learned how an illness could change a life.

On successive Fridays, Dr. Schubert, a pediatrician with interest in the gastrointestinal system, introduced us to two patients. The first was an infant whose liver lacked small channels called ducts. The condition, called biliary atresia, was associated with stunted growth, liver enlargement, a persistent yellow-green coloration of the skin (jaundice) and passage of pale stools. The infant in Dr. Schubert's arms produced a sample of stool as if on cue. The infant's diaper was passed among us.

The next week, Dr. Schubert talked of Hirschsprungs disease, a condition where the bowel lacks in one segment a necessary nerve supply. The infant afflicted with the condition can not easily pass stools. Once the disease is discovered, the bowel segment is surgically removed and the patient is provided a colostomy where stool is diverted out the front of the abdomen and collected in an ostomy bag. After the patient and their bowel has grown, the ostomy is removed and the bowel is reconstructed such that the stool is again passed through the rectum. Dr. Schubert discussed these medical details while a nine- year-old patient with Hirschsprungs disease stood at his side. At an appropriate time, without hesitation, she lifted her dress and modeled her plastic ostomy bag. As a result of these two Friday encounters, I marveled at the frailty and innocence of children.

Children had long held my fascination.

I HOPE THAT YOURS WILL BE THE SAME

She determined the grace and gait
Of the chestnut animal
And directed his final steps
To the center of the ring
Where wooden boxes, steeped in dung
Permitted her single boot
To reach a solid structure
Still four feet from the ground.
Not burdened with his rein in her hand
She led him to the southernmost stall,
Impervious to the legs and rumps
That towered all around.
Angered by his slow response
To abide the command to enter,
She slapped him on the thigh

Then looked toward us from under the hat
That held those curls from freedom.
She smiled as she hobbled past,
And explained the reason for the cast:
"Duke stepped on my foot Sunday."

ATTRACTION VS EXCLUSION

Since patient experiences were infrequent early on, little other than book work could color your perception of medicine. As a standard to this day, students rotated on an in-patient basis through all the disciplines. In four week to twelve week blocks, students temporarily took on the life of a practicing physician who concentrated on one area of medicine.

As a student, you followed a set pattern. You arrived at the hospital at dawn and stayed until dinner time caring for your hospitalized patients. You accepted no admissions. This was referred to as a no-call day. On the second day you arrived at 7 AM, cared for your own patients and accepted new admissions to the hospital until 4 PM. This was a short-call day. A late admission, say beyond 3 PM on a short-call day would assure you a missed dinner and a later than usual departure from the hospital. On the third day, you arrived before breakfast. At 8 AM you were "on-call" for the next 24 hours. During this time you accepted new admissions to the hospital. At 5 PM other students and physicians in training left you to care for all the hospitalized patients. During the 24 hours of call, you rarely had a chance to be off your feet. You had to retain your mental powers despite the fatigue. You were thankful your colleagues returned the next morning. At 8 AM you were then "post-call" and in the hospital until dinner time. Unbathed, unshaven, and exhausted, you were freed after being on your feet for 30 hours. When no one died on your watch, and you survived another emotional and physical battle, prayer was common.

INVOCATION

Oh Lord, grant through your infinite powers
A blessing of peace on this assembly of graduates
And those who come to share their joyous hour.
We raise our hats to everything they have accomplished to date
And roll up our sleeves to work for their tomorrows.
We ask that the beam from your medicinal star
Shine brightly on their patients, young and old.
Please grant these Docs the unfaltering trust to call 'em right
On the basis of a history and physical examination.
As a group, may they find continued fellowship
Despite geographic dispersal at months end.
Lastly, we ask that you retain us all under your curtain of embracing love
And bare closer to the residents' hearts the wishes of life's bounty;
For they have sacrificed, delayed rewards,
And, short of you, spent far too many nights on-call.

Reprinted with permission from *Annals of Emergency Medicine* 22:1491,1993

The idea behind this structured regimen was to provide medical students with a well-rounded knowledge of inpatient care in primary care fields (Family Practice, Internal Medicine, OB-Gyn, Pediatrics) or subspecialty care (such as Surgery, Radiology, Anesthesia, etc.). When an area struck your fancy, you were then given an opportunity to concentrate your fourth year studies in that subject. The educational concept was to drive you to a life-long pursuit of an area of attraction. For me, the sequential exposure drove me away from something. The first I dismissed was Surgery.

NO THANKS TO SURGERY

Within hours of joining the surgical team, we evaluated a middle-aged woman for abdominal pain. Her pain was severe, and it was obvious that my supervising physicians felt she had a catastrophic event that necessitated going to the operating room. I was clueless to the cause of her pain. My chief resident ("chief"), who was in his 6th and last year of general surgical training, suggested she likely had appendicitis. She also had a predisposition to blood vessel disturbances because of an underlying disease, called lupus. The anesthesiologist was contacted. He obliged the chief by knocking her out in the operating room. The chief cut through the abdominal tissue planes I had memorized in anatomy class. He found her appendix normal. Then he pulled every inch of her bowel out of its cavity. While examining every surface, finding it to be normal, I could only admire the glistening surfaces and the vibrant colors. Whereas the chief was perplexed and deeply disturbed to find nothing wrong with her entire abdominal contents, I was fascinated by my direct observations and proximity to living tissue. The chief closed her abdominal cavity up and she was transferred to the recovery room. She died 20 minutes later. I immediately recognized it was both hazardous to have lupus and maybe to be a surgeon.

Before I recovered from the shock of the fatality, the chief sent me into see the first admission for my surgical on call day. The gentleman was an active grandfather with a passion for the Cincinnati Redlegs. He had 20 pounds of weight loss from spring training to the All-Star break. He had lost his appetite and had a particular aversion for meats. The chief had felt a midline upper abdominal mass, but I could discern nothing unusual when I felt the patient's wasted profile. At operation the following day, I held the grandfather's skin and abdominal muscles with retractors, uncovering an advanced stomach cancer that was deemed inoperable. The grandfather never saw the Big Red Machine in its glory. By the second sunset on my life as surgeon, I sensed sudden death could be advantageous. I also recognized I needed to enhance my sense of touch in an all-important physician's implement, fingertips.

THE LIGHT OF EXPERIENCE

Wisdom was gained when meeting the light
With walking stick in hand.
The ashen shaft partook of the dew
Which trickled from stem to stem.
With every step it caressed the path
Which lay in darkness still,
To ascertain the life therein
And thank it for its sacrifice.

Unemotional, technical virtuosity is the hallmark of a good surgeon. I failed that measure repeatedly. A fellow with lung cancer developed labored breathing. He needed drainage of fluid from around his lung. In the treatment room, the supervising first-year resident (also known as an intern) prepared the needles and drapes while instructing me on the steps for what is called a thoracentesis. I picked up the sterile gloves awkwardly and contaminated two different pairs before I successfully "gloved." I leaned over my sterile field and my tie swept across and contaminated the third pair of gloves. The intern summarily told me I was done. Fellow student Rick Sieving gloved on his first effort. Rick pushed and pushed the needle but couldn't get the tip through the gentleman's chest wall. Suddenly, the needle disappeared as Rick drove the 3 ½ " needle 3" further than it should have been passed. Rick uttered, "Whoops," which is an obvious admission no patient wishes to hear. The man screamed in either fright or pain. He was able to breathe better after the fluid was released. Apparently, Rick speared nothing critical.

Rick Sieving became a heart specialist, who as an interventional cardiologist concentrates on delicate procedures such as coronary artery catheterization. During my own brief, unexplained episode of chest pain in early 1980, I sought Rick out. His hands had long improved. On the other hand, my surgical skills remained rudimentary.

We were assigned to the Emergency Department (E.D.) under the supervision of a surgical resident in order to sew up lacerations.

Theoretically, the surgical resident and an E.D. nurse were always available, but both were scarce. We were assigned a one-week schedule where we were working 12 hours on duty, 12 hours off, 12 hours on and 24 hours off. My first patient was a housewife who severely cut the tip of her ring finger while discarding a green bean can lid. I set out all the equipment I thought was needed and injected the numbing agent, Lidocaine, in four spots at the base of her finger where pain nerves are located. I infiltrated the medicine for this nerve block and waited the standard five minutes. Because she could still feel pain, I injected a second time, giving ultimately twice the standard volume of Lidocaine for a nerve block. I waited an additional five minutes to no avail. She felt every stitch I made over the next 15 minutes. When I was done torturing her, I kicked open the suture room door. Four wide-eyed patients in need of my stitching were clustered on a narrow bench. My patient held her newly bandaged finger, demonstrably waving the wound in the air and energetically blurted, "He's a butcher; he killed me!" I had to change my scrub suit shirt as the arm pits were drenched and I had more than eleven hours to go in the shift.

Thankfully, I was spared uninvited feedback on my first episiotomy repair. The resident had created the episiotomy (a controlled laceration) on a woman who was delivering an infant very rapidly. The surgeon cut from the lower half of the patient's vagina toward the area between her groin crease and rectum. The controlled cut prevented uncontrolled tearing of her tissues. After an uneventful delivery, I was told to sew things back together even though I had never seen this done before. In 30 minutes I had somehow created a residual 1" redundant flap at her right vaginal lip. The young woman could have lent her opinion of my handiwork only if she had a mirror to look at the reflected image of her now-altered vagina. Because she went home within hours of delivering an infant, only the resident who viewed my Mark Chagal-like artistry recognized the error. Thirty years later she could not recognize me, but if I saw her vagina today, I'd recognize the unnatural creation.

NO WINS IN INTERNAL MEDICINE

Technical prowess is not the forte of general Internal Medicine (I.M.). The prized internist has perfect recall for even the most obtuse facts. The superior internist has the capacity to ferret out the cause of any complaint or combination of complaints. When the history of the present illness or physical examination leave the internist unsettled, he or she resorts to analysis of laboratory data. The internist who capably interprets the history, physical and laboratory information is held in great esteem.

On my first on-call night in Internal Medicine, I ordered a urine specimen on a modestly confused gentleman with a high fever as a result of his urinary tract infection.

"There is nothing wrong with me Doc, 'cept I'm a Disabled American Veteran," he said.

I gave him a sterile cup, directed him to place his specimen in the cup. He returned from the cupboard-sized hospital bathroom straight-faced, holding the cup filled with coughed-up phlegm (sputum). And no lie, the next admitted patient had pneumonia. I gave him a container for a sputum specimen. After I told him to cough up phlegm, he urinated in the cup! I disqualified myself from I.M. for failing to grasp the basic principles of the discipline.

On the second on-call night, a patient was admitted for repeated vomiting. Because his stomach eventually bled, at 2 AM I had to pass a nasogastric tube in the ward treatment room. This is a pencil-thick, 3' long, flexible hose. The nasogastric (ng) tube can get caught at normal places or end up in abnormal places such as the brain or a lung, neither of which is good for the patient. In order to get the ng tube to where it is supposed to go, you have the patient first sit upright. You pass the tube into the patient's nostril. After ascending 3" into the far reaches of the nose, the tube rests at the back of the throat. The tube must then make a gigantic turn and now descend downward toward the stomach. However, as you push, the tube typically continues upward, striking the back of the throat and causing the patient to gag. I was at this stage of resistance with my gagging patient. I called my shepherd, the supervising resident. He arrived in crumbled clothing bearing a weary appearance. The resident asked the patient to open his mouth. The resident looked at the nasogastric tube which was in the back of throat, pointing in the wrong direction. He told the patient to swallow, then abruptly jammed the tube into the patient's stomach. The resident gave me a look that would kill, then left without comment. Two sheep remained in the room.

Patients with complex problems threw me for a loop. I stumbled through establishing the diagnosis of acutely ill hospitalized patients while on the I.M. service. Despite soliciting assistance from all available avenues, I could not coordinate effective treatment. As an example, one elderly gentleman was found mid-afternoon unresponsive on his boarding room floor. He was admitted and remained confused. I gave him intravenous digitalis repeatedly overnight for an abnormal heart rhythm. By morning his heart rhythm stabilized, but his blood work that morning showed that he was anemic. In searching for possible blood loss, I performed a rectal examination. He appeared to have advanced prostate cancer. By lunch (which I missed) he partially lost muscle tone and became unconscious from what appeared to be a stroke. That afternoon, he oozed blood from small razor nicks on his face from the needed barbering done that morning by an aide. By dinner time, I arranged for a blood specialist called a hematologist to perform a bone marrow biopsy. The biopsy was successfully performed on the back of the patient's hip, but when we turned him over, a hernia popped out in his groin. I couldn't get the strangled loop of bowel out of his scrotal sac. I called a surgeon on the Emergency Service, who would not operate as the patient was too great a surgical risk. Since I was post-call, I signed my newest patient and other hospitalized patients under my care over to the next on-call physician.

Ruth and I were in the midst of our courtship. She had prepared a candlelight dinner for 6 PM. I got home at 9 PM, lost my own muscle tone and fell asleep in the bathtub.

NEITHER G.P. NOR F.P. OK

Family Practice (F.P.) is now the preferred term for what in my day was called the General Practitioner (G.P.). The F.P. physician spends three years beyond medical school taking care of both sexes, all ages, including newborn infants and geriatric patients. The family practitioner in the course of care stresses health lifestyles, screens often for detectable diseases, treats ailments and, most importantly, knows the family members as if they are kin. The time I met three of these qualifying characteristics of a family practitioner, I cared for Mr. Ballor.

William Ballor was a life-long resident of Clifton Heights, a lower-income community totally surrounding the University of Cincinnati. After our marriage, despite the protest of my in-laws, Ruth and I paid $110 for occupying the second floor of a narrow row house in Clifton Heights. Every third night, I was in-hospital on call. Ruth slept those nights in clothing and maintained her untied shoes at the base of her bed. She mentally rehearsed her exit. She would climb out the front window, descend to the ground via the porch bannister, and drive off if she heard a burglar within her house.

William Ballor was in the hospital because his cirrhotic, failing liver was injured from years of drinking. Another alcoholic hospitalized two days before on our floor went into kidney failure and liver failure, in part because the residents tried to get too much fluid out of her system too fast. We were cautiously reducing Mr. Ballor's excess body fluids and he was on our service for weeks. I found out he lived one block from me. Like many individuals who often drink, Mr. Ballor told great stories. I was pleased to see him in clinic after his successful hospital discharge.

Several months later on a Saturday evening, Mr. Ballor vomited blood. At 3:10 AM he called our house. Ruth answered Mr. Ballor's request for me, "He is not here now, but I expect him at any minute," another rehearsed response. Following her suggestion that vomiting blood was a reason to go to the hospital, Mr. Ballor complied. I was of course on-call, and Mr. Ballor was admitted to my care by 4:00 AM. With the help of my supervisor resident, we placed a standard ng tube in his nose. A second, special tube was inflated in his stomach, suspended on weights and supported by the face mask of a football helmet. This archaic method to stem the blood from esophageal varices did not prevent him from bleeding. At noon, after nineteen units of blood, my attending physician, the individual ultimately responsible for all the residents and students, suggested that I had to cut off precious blood replacement at some point. I asked to give one more unit if necessary. The attending concurred. I left the Intensive Care Unit to smoke a cigarette, even though I didn't smoke. I prayed for Mr. Ballor to die peacefully. Shortly after receiving the twentieth unit, Mr. Ballor became agitated, largely because he knew he was dying. I administered a low dose of intravenous valium. He stopped breathing and shared no further stories. I vowed never again to be this close to anyone while providing their medical care.

USHERING THE INTRODUCTION TO ANCESTRY

Dead right there is the provider's depiction
In the prehospital setting of a certainty.
In transit, protocols devised to salvage
Are carried out half-hearted or incompletely.
Our pronouncement will be but formality;
The certificate, a stiff subpoena to their ancestry.
This introduction may be without E.D. ceremony;
Many surrender their last breath to other trustees.
However, we're likely to encounter those precipitously
Struck by pneumococcus, thrombus, vehicle, and O.D.,
Or lamed by blade, missile, and betrayed
By a chronic affliction or the serenity of a crib.
For these uninvited, who are welcomed at our trauma bays
We're invariably rehearsed and temperamentally driven
To secure airway patency and access central veins.
Beyond ABC's we're a group as diverse as non-perfusing rhythms;
While some are consumed by the mechanical things

Others mentate and reflect upon the spiritual cascades.
Ultimately, we will address the surviving fated
To grieve for a loss, we too withstood.
How we process and react to cries that penetrate
The air and our minds determines the likelihood
That energizing strength, us both regenerates.
Blessed are those who grow from a death encounter.

Reprinted with permission from *Academic Emergency* Medicine 2:528,1995.

PSYCH TOO CRAZY

For the four-week exposure to the discipline of mental health, I was assigned two preceptors who were practicing psychiatrists. The more gifted physician was in charge of an inpatient Psychiatric Unit at a Catholic-owned community hospital. Dr. McMann was accustomed to medical students and relished his role as a teacher. However, his administrative responsibilities within the hospital cut down on our contact time. I spent as many or more hours in the accompaniment of Sister Constance, who was a psychiatric social worker.

Sister led daily group mental health sessions for the 10-12 patients who were housed on the Unit at any given time. Most who were hospitalized had consented for inpatient management of either a new problem, or an exacerbation of a chronic problem. They were given attention by the multi-disciplinary Unit team for one week to one month, depending upon the severity and nature of their illness. There was a more rapid turnover of patients who were "pink-sheeted." A person who had become unmanageable by their family or were deemed too unstable by family or co-workers could be involuntarily committed (probated) for 72 hours on the Psych Unit upon filling out a form that was pink in color.

Although the "lock ups" I witnessed appeared justified, anyone could fill out a pink sheet, effectively taking someone from their routine. Within three business days, Dr. McMann was responsible for assessing stability of their mental health. He and the retained patient would then appear before a Probate Court judge. The person who filled the pink sheet told the judge their thoughts, and the person probated gave a rebuttal. Dr. McMann presented the psychiatric summary that came from his interview sessions and the assembled profiles of the Unit staff. The judge would either free the person to the street or commit them to further hospitalization at the community hospital or Longview State Hospital if they were uninsured.

The Probate Court I saw several times per week was horrifying. The judge resided on an elevated platform. The probated patient sat below in the first row of a series of fixed benches. There was no separation from others who were free to assemble anywhere in the room. People hung out in open doorways at either side of the judge. An obese armed guard at the rear of the room overtly flirted with the court recorder. Both were oblivious to the rancor about them. The back of the room was part of the foot traffic pattern for the public seeking Domestic Court hearings. While perfect strangers milled, someone's future was debated and determined.

Trips with Dr. McMann to Hamilton County Jail were also horrifying, but for a different reason. I felt a certain uneasiness the first time mechanically-driven bars or doors brought me into the confines of incarcerated people. Although I physically cringed less with repeat visits, I remained uncomfortable, even though we never made it into the depths of the jail cells. Typically, guards sequestered the newly-admitted prisoners in a side room and provided us all seats around a table. Dr. McMann sat across from the prisoner, and depending upon the nature of the alleged offense, questions varied. While assessing a serial thief, Dr. McMann once asked, "What does the following statement mean? The grass is always greener on the other side of the fence."

The prisoner replied, "If no one is looking, you can take what's on the other side of the fence."

As good as Dr. McMann was, Sister Constance was better. She placed patients at ease with a gentle smile and non-confrontational body language. She interviewed you, and you didn't know she extracted secrets, collated your information to make an accurate assessment of your sanity. I willingly lent her my thoughts and heart as I was being challenged during this time frame by the Catholic Church. I had to complete New Testament readings, respond in writing to interrogatories and meet weekly with Father Bill Williams. The individual sessions were prerequisites for marrying Ruth. I had to contractually consent to raise my children as Catholics. I had to pass the Father's scrutiny. Apparently, I fared better than Father Bill. I subsequently married Ruth with the Church's blessing but Father left the priesthood. He was a sane man who was confused and disillusioned by the Church's persistent rigidity on certain issues and equally appalled by Vatican II, which destroyed tradition.

THE MOST REVEREND

The old country was his mother
Of kindness, comfort, and shelter.
Infant pathways had never changed;
There was but one season temperate
With two candles on the Sabbath
And grace before three meals.
How unjust, too inclement
Were human needs and wants.

Had Father Williams sought attention from Dr. McMann, the support would have sustained his mental health. Had Father seen Dr. Joe Welkin, my other psychiatric preceptor, both would have been in trouble. Dr. Welkin was not conscious of his own limitations and could do little to ameliorate the suffering of others. As an example, when one of Dr. Welkin's patients hospitalized with depression told Dr. Welkin she was having trouble having a bowel movement, he subjected her to an upper gastrointestinal series and a barium enema. She simply needed a laxative.

The ills of Dr. Welkin more than neutralized the positive impact Dr. McMann had on my career choice. Psychiatry provided an enticing aroma of assistance to people distressed from the demands of life. The practice seemed intellectually seductive. Ultimately, the inexactness of the trade was too troubling.

ORTHOPEDICS, MORE EXACTING

Those interested in orthopedics complete an internship year of general surgery training. They then complete four additional years in an orthopedic residency. In the course of endless hours of training, they learn to assess and treat a myriad of musculoskeletal complaints. Jokes had long depicted orthopedic physicians as hairy-knuckled individuals with large arms and small cranial vaults. During my medical school days, the field did attract muscular guys with seemingly high testosterone levels. They seemed bright enough to me and for whatever reasons, well suited to the tools of the trade. They could hammer, chisel, and saw with the precision of the most talented wood working craftsmen. I was envious of their skills, yet I could not overcome the violence of orthopedic acts.

After the one week experience in the suture room, we were assigned a one week exposure to Emergency Surgery. On the rotation, I trailed a surgical intern, a surgical chief resident and an orthopedic resident. They responded to the needs of patients in the Emergency Department who had presented with surgical complaints and evaluated hospitalized patients who developed a problem amenable to surgical intervention. One evening we were called to the E.D. to care for a victim of an automobile accident. A middle-aged gentleman left the Interstate en route to his house, and a drunk driver wrongly entered the same ramp. As a result of the head-on collision, the intoxicated person was uninjured. The innocent victim struck his head on the window and his knee on the dash. He was knocked unconscious for a brief time and sustained a large forehead cut. The impact on the knee was transmitted to the long bone in his thigh (femur). All other body parts had been assessed uninjured by the E.D. staff. After injecting the scalp with numbing medication, I repaired the laceration. At the same time, the orthopedic resident tended to the fractured femur. The orthopedic resident drilled, then terminally hammered a rod from one skin edge through the lower part of the femur bone and out the other skin edge. From the rod, he affixed a series of pulleys and weights to suspend the fractured femur. The resident performed the procedures without any numbing medications, sedatives or pain-relieving medicines. He indicated he wanted the man to be awake and alert so that the status of his head injury could be serially observed.

The mellowness and impregnable cool of the orthopedic resident while fashioning all appliances was in one sense admirable, but at the same time, was incredibly cruel. As a student, I lent no criticism of him. Feeling the reverberant screams, I wished the now twice-injured man could return the pain to the orthopedic resident.

I soon learned that even when the orthopedic torture was silenced by general anesthesia, I still felt the pain. This was apparent for another victim of an automobile collision. In the course of a sideswiping accident, a woman sustained a severe laceration to her arm. Broken glass had created a 12" cut to her forearm. There was also a partial amputation of the ring finger. Due to the extent of her injuries, she was taken to the operating room. The orthopedic resident started at one end of the laceration, and I started at the other end of the laceration. We met at the middle, then the orthopedic resident turned to me for repair of her injured finger. He handed me a bone rongeur and told me to use the instrument to snip off ¼" of her exposed bone. After the bone was cut back, he would then create a flap of skin to cover the shortened finger. I shuttered while I snipped off the bone under what had been her fingernail and was grateful that I did not pass out.

TRIALS AS A PATHOLOGIST

When crisp leaves were in short supply to burn, I gently thumped ants into submission, focused the beam of a magnifying glass and incinerated them while alive. This elementary school pastime was synonymous with evening swatting of fire flies with a fungo bat. You could drive a fading flicker of luminescence 6-8' with a well-centered strike. These revolting activities rivaled the adrenalin rush of igniting a hanging wasp comb with a kerosene-soaked rag on a broom handle. A most natural advancement to these activities was targeting back yard schools of roosting birds with air guns. Pop had prohibited us from igniting fireworks and shooting air guns, but both were in great supply in our neighborhood. Sandy Youkalis, down the block, with whom we played never-ending Monopoly games, would trade lighted cherry bombs for anyone foolish enough to give him an apple on Halloween, and he had plenty of incendiaries in reserve. Denny Staub, our neighbor, had an air rifle that brother and I coveted. One afternoon behind the Hankes garage, when we tired of targeting tin cans, I purposefully fired at a treed robin. He alighted, flew for a few seconds and fell to the ground. I watched him gasp his last breath and knew from that moment on I wished to never be responsible for causing death.

A SUNRISE BURIAL

For everlasting the stream will wash
The life born scents below the pyre.
Motionless now it lies before her
And before her eyes it will expire.
Needless now are the wings for speed
The flight to heaven will soon proceed.

In Dr. Spear's college physiology course, my lab partner had to sacrifice the living frogs. I could perform the experiments on muscle membrane action potentials without recoiling. I could also do the dissection of preserved frogs in Mr. Woodward's high school Biology class, and the shark, pig and cat in college Comparative Anatomy. These animals were dead, and in theory, they felt no pain.

Pathologists did not kill the patients they dissected. Pathologists were not responsible for the patients' terminal events. In fact, the pathologist played a role in potentially postponing in other patients the inevitable sequence of death. Routinely, during my medical school days, one quarter of patients who died were "posted." The pathologist was requested to perform a post-mortem examination ("a post") in order to enlighten the treating clinician. The pathologist would uncover with regularity a diseased organ or medical condition that was hidden from the patient's treating physician. The pathologist would have the operator page over the loud speaker, "Doctor's post," to summon all interested clinicians to the dissecting table. I found these post-mortem lessons indispensable, even when I had no previous contact with the patient.

I was slow to appreciate the talents of pathologists and the not-so-silent messages they could convey. Like my other fellow medical students, my introduction to their work was a mandated assignment. As part of our second year Pathology course instruction, we had to attend four separate post-mortem examinations (autopsies) and write up four Autopsy Reports. These structured reports detailed the patient's clinical course and speculations the clinician wrote in the patient's chart. This information was extracted from the patient's medical record and the "Death Note" written by the treating doctor. The information preceded the results of the post-mortem findings uncovered by the pathologist. Such a report necessitated access to a type writer and consumed at least two to three hours of precious time. Additional time was spent trying to find impending autopsies. They had to be performed after class time instruction or on weekends. You found yourself morbidly calling all over the city to see if anyone died.

IN RESPONSE TO HIS POST

Midline stroke, sternum to pubis.
Tickle tummy with forceful skill.
No breath, no giggle.
Exploration to teach us five
Gathered under the light
To see what took his life.
His heart, his heart–
Look at this heart.
No? Not so, the fluid in the lungs.
It bathes a hidden growth
Once nurtured by tobacco.

Two polyps in the gut,
The bladder filled with blood.
He's dead, one paper says it so.
He lived, another said it so.

Many post-mortem examinations were carried out at the Hamilton County Morgue and at the University Hospital, which was our main teaching facility. The autopsies at the morgue were generally performed on healthy, young people who died as a result of self-inflicted violence or died precipitously at the hands of a spouse, from the events of an escalated neighborly quarrel, a bad drug deal or an accident. The Autopsy Reports from these deaths were brief and easy to write up. It was a challenge to beat one of your classmates to one of these posts. On the other hand, Dr. Cleveland, the County Coroner, also posted long-deceased individuals whose bodies were in various stages of decay. The clerk at the morgue performed beyond her capacity as a civil servant. To our inquiries, "Any deaths?" she might add, "Yes, but it's a floater from the Ohio River. You don't want to come." We didn't.

Posts were also performed at each of Cincinnati's area hospitals. You were drawn to or repelled from these posts more by the pathologist than from the patient's mechanism of death. Dr. Jolly possessed the hands of a surgeon and radiated infectious enthusiasm. He attracted medical as well as nursing students. He provided continuous pearls to anyone in attendance and typically provoked the audience seeking to elicit a fainting episode in an observer. Dr. Altshueler found every case unique, no matter how mundane the events seemed to others. His effervescence wore thin on his fellow coworkers. Dr. Jan Schwartz possessed a photographic memory and reveled at knowing everything there was to know about infectious diseases, especially fungal infections. He freely lectured in a thick Austrian accent offering tidbits such as, "*Histoplasmosis gondii* infection predominantly occurs in man, and other forms of lower animals, if there were anything in this world lower than man." No one possessed a more encyclopedic knowledge of pathology than Dr. Ed Gall. He could detail 50 different afflictions of the lung that could kill, yet he chained smoked. His colleague, Dr.

Wozenkrantz, despite constantly coughing up phlegm from one of those 50 conditions, saccular bronchiectasis, smoked as well. In contrast, because he was health conscious and believed in its medicinal value, Dr. Mandeburg daily luncheoned on and constantly reeked of garlic. Mandeburg's area of expertise was neuropathology, the study of the brain. With his halting, old country speech and slovenly appearance, when in proximity to Dr. Mandeburg, you anticipated encountering Boris Karloff.

When the four mandated autopsies provoked my attentions, I elected to take a position offered at the Department of Pediatric Pathology. Over the three months between my second and third year of medical school, I worked with a select group of pediatric pathologists. They were all professors within the university. They worked closely with the clinical specialists such as the surgeon or tumor specialist (oncologist) to promptly identify removed tumor tissues. Each pathologist had a specific area of interest. As an example, Dr. Kevin Bove spent his available waking moments on establishing the causes of pediatric muscle disease. Dr. A. James McAdams concentrated on the kidney. In their decades of tireless work, they uncovered many of the complexities of childhood kidney and muscle ailments. The two wrote hundreds of scientific papers and were known throughout the world for their expertise. Not uncommonly, the Department would be shipped from great distance muscle or kidney specimens for these two to examine.

All the pediatric pathologists performed autopsies on children. Every one of the pathologists except Jim McAdams wore protective gown and surgical gloves during the performance of an autopsy. Jim performed the post-mortem examination bare-handed and bow-tied. All the pathologists tutored me on the various techniques they had found to be most useful. They taught me how to obtain appropriate tissue sections. They attempted to teach me how to interpret the processed tissues affixed to a slide under a microscope. Unfortunately, I was a slow learner. In the first day they assigned me slides to interpret from a previously performed autopsy. It took me close to a week to identify the 40 specimens. I had difficulty determining which piece of tissue was lung, which was brain, or liver, etc. When I did figure out what the identity of a specimen was, I had little confidence in my ability to define what, if anything, was wrong with the piece of tissue. By summer's end, I had made advancement. The day before I permanently retired as a pediatric pathologist, my replacement arrived. Dr. Larry Sarff was given a tray with 40 unknown tissue slides. Despite having six years more education than I, he turned to me to assist his identification of lung from liver!

I admired many aspects of pathology. Pathologists had important service roles that benefitted patients. They advanced scientific knowledge of various disease states. They potentially helped all clinicians by their publications, especially with a form of writing, the pathologists referred to as a clinicopathologic conference (C.P.C.). The C.P.C.'s consistent form expressed the opinions of the treating physician followed by the pathologist's ultimate findings.

Although pathologists had patient contact, it was not the quality of contact that could sustain my interest.

THE ACTION FIELD OF EMERGENCY MEDICINE

Contact I did desire was available within the confines of an Emergency Department.

E-CODE FOR THE SEASONS

Stalactited crystals on the Emergency sign
Despite any ornamental beauty, are virulent.
You'll soon meet a senior unwittingly assigned
To the spiraling plummet of independence
Who's lost both balance and a lesser trochanter.
The event is equally educational and stressful
For the adolescent who poorly negotiated an incline
Splintered with stumps on a rudimentary device
Who's sustained a solid organ, subcapsular bleed.
Weather's not a cofactoring issue at August end

As six-year-olds first leave their protective nests.
The harbinger may be a digit in pencil sharpener
Or the sacrifice of a long bone in a dart
Between parked cars at the bus stop depot.
Though the lessens for us are less predictable,
School opening joins summer-fall-winter-spring.

Reprinted with permission from *Academic Emergency Medicine* 5:8,1998.

My earliest experiences in an E.D. were from the consumer side. Two events have stuck with me.

When I was an adolescent, my younger sister, Mickie, took a dive from a piece of playground equipment. From the deformity and her degree of pain, it was obvious that she had sustained a fracture of the elbow. We hustled her to the E.D. and they did a great job of treating her and placating our anxiety.

When Mom was menopausal, she had periods of heavy vaginal bleeding. One afternoon when bleeding was excessive, Pop climbed in the back seat of the Plymouth holding the towel Mom quickly soaked with blood, and at their direction, I sped to the hospital emergency entrance. I dropped them off. They filled out the requisite papers, and both were in the waiting room when I returned from the parking garage. Father repeated his desire for the nurse behind the desk to expedite Mom's care. Nothing happened. After several minutes, he reached over the barrier, grabbed the woman by her collar, elevated her from her sitting position and said, "My wife's hemorrhaging, and I want her to see the doctor *now*!" Pop sat her back down, and as her eyes returned to their sockets, she placed two urgent calls. The treating physician, who was not present in the department, and security officer both promptly arrived. The physician arrested Mom's bleeding and the officer declined to arrest father.

Since 1975, a time when first graduates of formal Emergency Medicine training went forth to care for emergency patients, the staff of the E.D. has been present 24 hours daily. Our families' needs and others like us have been well served by the talents of the administrative staff, nurses and physicians who've delighted in rendering care in the Emergency Department setting. They have evaluated and treated any and all illnesses or injuries accepting the fragility of life.

BALANCING DETAILS FROM OUR MEMORY

Rusted screws on the handle base welded by rain
Were fracture-repaired by mythological fixation.
An aluminum sheet remarsupialized the frame.
The axle transferred control to replacement wheels.
This genomic hybridization you have fathered
Should long ago been rejected at a yard sale.
Yet, this lumbering cart remains your cranial vessel.
Within the carriage you placed flash card queries.
The wooden slats initially corralled "The Cat in the Hat".
Subsequently, the flatbed's been laden with scientific theory.
Tonight you draw this creaking chariot across our finish line
In order to receive a framable garland of completion.
When you retrieve and manipulate from your depot
Interconnecting facts that solve ED complexities
Recall that life is as fragile as your Radio Flyer.

Reprinted with permission from *Academic Emergency Medicine* 3:688, 1996.

As a medical student, we could volunteer to spend a month functioning in the role of an emergency physician. By and large, I found this elective experience intellectually challenging. You faced people with undifferentiated complaints (such as deformed elbow, or vaginal bleeding), and it was your responsibility to ferret out the cause of the ailment and define a treatment plan. With correct judgement, you could often see immediate patient improvements with your therapy and know that you impacted someone's outcome. Relief of patient symptoms or a family member's smile brought instant gratification.

The downside of Emergency Medicine practice was an overemphasis on patients with alcohol-related problems and contact with mentally-impaired people under the influence of illicit drugs. We also evaluated too many patients who were victims of domestic violence or random assault. These horrors occurred in the community the University Hospital served, including the E.D. lobby.

A mother brought her child to the E.D. for evaluation of a respiratory illness. For reasons I did not know, the mother quarreled with the father. Events escalated as I chose the medical record from the chart rack. When I entered the treatment room, the mother was in the process of burying the pump heel of her shoe in the back of his head. He went unconscious before me from a depressed skull fracture.

A pregnant woman seeking medical attention for feet swelling encountered her future child's father in the E.D. lobby. He was in the accompaniment of another woman suffering a complication of pregnancy. The women uncovered the conjoint father's deception and one woman withdrew a gun from her purse and shot the other woman in the uterus.

In the month I experienced, bullet holes seemed to be contagious. You rarely knew enough about how they got there. When presented with more than one victim simultaneously, you wanted to save the good guy before the bad guy, but the information from silenced people rarely came. You were left to imagine that no such events could befall you or your family.

On weekend evenings, if injured people were not shot, they were stabbed. If verbal, the stabbed victim would indicate they were humbly minding their own business and some "dude" cut them. Occasionally, there was a history. "Henry got angry and he started to beat me so I stabbed him." Before Henry's lung collapsed, he had enough fight left to wrench free the knife and half cut off his wife's ear. They were adjacent to each other in the treatment area and seemingly concerned about each other's progress.

UNCERTAIN RUSTLING OF THE CURTAINS

Inadvertently pruned at bar's closure by some "dude"
This partially anesthetized spirit joins the stockpot
Of souls who arrive past midnight that triage will conclude
Can be sequenced and until then corralled at ear shot.
Failing to recess despite the hour, detained penitents
Restore their fever for life from our rotating ministry.
Patients have missed appointments, couldn't sleep, had an accident
And look to us with absolute certainty to define their difficulty breathing.
Despite the salvation that more than occasionally transpires
The majority of our curtain rustling does not uncover
Hidden agendas or diagnoses despite the ICD-9 codifiers.
Few parishioners in our trust lament; our caring is not a veneer.

Reprinted with Permission from *Academic Emergency Medicine* 2:850,1995.

Blood was typically everywhere. By month's end I had contracted hepatitis B from one or several bloody encounters. Upon recovering, I swore off adult emergency medicine.

INTRODUCTION TO PEDIATRIC EMERGENCY MEDICINE

Whereas adults in E.D.s often abused themselves and others, violated acts of nature, and sought relief from circumstances they potentially could have avoided with minimal intelligent forethought, children suffered from events that were often out of their control. With the help of Drs. Ed Donovan and Bill Balistreri, when I first stepped foot in the area of the E.D. reserved for children, I felt purged of adult evils. Here were innocents symptomatic from unexpected illness or injury. They pleaded for your undivided attention.

When you walked into the treatment room of an adult, you introduced yourself formally. The adult patient knew in principle your role, and because they often waited awhile in the E.D. getting to you, they were generally relieved with your arrival, even if you were a medical student. I was quick to appreciate when you walked into the space surrounding a child in the E.D., they instinctively knew you were a physician equivalent. Your role was to inflict pain. You were going to administer a shot. They were not pleased to be in the environment of the E.D., and your introduction as a medical student was another threat. I watched many children, particularly those less than two years of age, who retreated to the confining arms of the person who brought them. Non-verbal and verbal behavior suggested distaste and terroristic fear of anyone who was a health care provider.

In order to counteract a child's aversion to a student doctor, I learned to walk into every encounter with a smile on my face. I developed a comforting style where I sought immediate eye contact with the pediatric patient. No matter what age or how rudimentary their communication skills, I wanted every child to know that they were my purpose for being there. Their illness was my illness to resolve. Their injury was mine to soothe. My non-verbal behavior and introduction was geared to reduce fear. The rewards were instantaneous.

OPENING EXCHANGES

Long fatigued by repetitive introductions
I slipped late evening into the doorway
To hear "Oh there's the doctor!"
I cringed, knowing our collective delay.
A three-year-old boy, chief complaint: foot injury
Rested anxiously on a nurturing lap.
His angry, dependent shoeless extremity
And feared expression clarified his mom's concern.
My eye caught a limp yellow companion
Silented by a timeworn grasp of its neck.
Its avian limbs pyramided on yet another lap.

My lead, "Who did you bring with you?"
"Duck", he replied quite naturally.
"Is that a small case 'd', or are we talking proper noun?"
"This is capital 'D", Duck," mom enjoined.
"Oh no," he corrected, "this is 'Ducky Wucky'."
Now I ask you all out there,
"How can you not love to care for kids?"

Reprinted with permission from *Academic Emergency Medicine* 6:53, 1998.

WARD TEAMS

Besides the patient contact, the attraction I felt toward a particular style of medicine was also influenced by the physicians who taught me. In the hospital setting, a medical student was part of a working unit, referred to as a team. A ward team was composed of individuals who were responsible for the care of up to 30-40 patients hospitalized on a specific floor or wing of the hospital. A ward team was lead by a 3rd year (senior) resident who supervised a 2nd year (junior) resident, one or two 1st year residents (interns), a 4th year medical student (junior intern) and three to four 3rd year medical students. A chief resident was over all senior residents. Attending physicians were responsible for the oversight of all residents in training.

The ward team assembled daily in pre-dawn hours for "working rounds." The senior coordinated the game plans for every hospitalized patient. With input from all the residents and the 4th year medical student, the senior determined who would benefit from additional studies, who needed changes in treatment, who required further hospitalization, and who could be discharged. Working rounds were conducted along with the head (charge) nurse in hallways outside the patient room. The senior was the nucleus of this beehive, and the 3rd year students were at the periphery, straining to hear the conversation and hoping for pearls of the educational exchange.

At the completion of working rounds, the 3rd year students were given specific patient responsibilities such as to draw blood from a vein (phlebotomy) or artery (blood gas), restart an intravenous line, place a nasogastric tube, etc. This was referred to as "scut work." The scut work theoretically benefited the patient. It definitely honed our technical skills. And, for many of us, carrying out painful procedures brought us perspective. For others, scut work was the formal induction to callousness.

"THE GAS" IN MAJOR 1

An excess of sixty years have passed
Before your cohorts committed
This gown unto my soul.
Enshroud a body in neutral-white
You may, yet contain you can't
This black integument of pride
Nor deflate, degrade the mind
By penetrance of that needle in your hand.
In health, I did not enter here,
But in health I wish to leave.
There is a life before me;
Much has remained unseen.
I only ask from you some dignity.
I know it's going to sting.

Reprinted with permission from *Journal of Emergency Medicine* 8:199,1990.

As a third-year student at the Veteran's Administration Hospital, when told to get a gas on a patient in the I.C.U. during work rounds, the junior resident addressed me abusively. He had received an award the week earlier for his clinical skills. The recognition as Intern of the Year suggested he had proved his worth to someone. However, I had known him for a few days and found him both arrogant and indifferent. He was discourteous to me and brief to the point of rudeness in responding to the patient who was trying to understand why he was struggling to breathe. I went to the senior resident at the end of rounds and vented my displeasure. I indicated that I refused to work in the presence of this prized physician, who I would be on call with for the next eleven weeks. The senior listened, modified that afternoon my future call dates and confided that he, too, had reservations about intelligence being over-prized compared to humanistic qualities.

Working rounds were traditionally abandoned on Sundays and holidays for ward teams. This was the case for my first on call date as a 3rd year student in the Neonatal Intensive Care Unit (N.I.C.U.). I introduced myself early Sunday morning to the senior resident. She signed a form and disappeared without comment. I read a textbook for three hours, ate lunch, then positioned myself in the physicians' lounge among an anesthesiologist and an OB-Gyn physician. Our football afternoon was interrupted by the unexpected labor of a woman who was not due for several months. She delivered a perfectly-formed, thin-skinned infant who weighed less than 1000 grams. In that year, survival rates for infants less than 1500 grams was close to zero. The infant made attempts to breathe. The mother was not given the opportunity to view the child. The child was transported to the N.I.C.U. and placed in a corner where the nurses ignored gasping respirations. When I asked why no one was intervening, I was advised to leave the child alone. My stimulation might prolong the spontaneous breathing or strengthen the heart rate. The infant had signs of life for another 30 minutes. The senior resident was contacted. She pronounced the child dead, filled out a death certificate and left the N.I.C.U., unresponsive to questions I had raised.

On Monday morning our attending physician, Dr. Rosemary Schmidt, conveyed her love of neonatal medicine. With her instruction and supervision over the month, we too would feel her enthusiasm. She suggested feedback on the teaching of the residents. I approached her in confidence regarding my previous day's experience. The complaint was taken seriously. Dr. Schmidt rectified suboptimal teaching by assigning me to a different resident. Later, I learned the resident in question was undergoing psychiatric treatment for new onset of depression.

In the late 1960s, medical supervisors were not dissimilar from supervisors in other industry. People at the top articulated the desire to be helpful and sought feedback. However, supervisors of medical students rarely solicited information, and when presented with a complaint, they rarely relished an opportunity to rectify a wrong. Third year medical students were the dogs in the family of medicine who were kicked to alleviate anxiety. Either because Dr. Schmidt could not tell me apart from fellow medical student Jim Finger or because she was different, Dr. Schmidt never retaliated for my indiscretion of complaining.

ATTENDING PHYSICIANS

There were many attending physicians from the community who helped shape medical students' patterns of medical practice. From exposure to literally hundreds of attending physicians, a select group have been my nourishment.

THE MONGOLOID CHILD

Moistened first are vertical shoots
While horizontals bear the weight
Until they yield to feed the roots.
Sodden boughs embrace the earth,
But stalwart limbs endure
The wind to be lightening struck.
A lusty child gets his mother's love
But it can not serve to supplement
Nature's rain and nourishment.

I admired all the attendings physicians who were willing to teach medical students and residents. Physicians who were in private practice sacrificed potential practice income by attending for a month on the ward. They consumed billable hours three to five times per week. They were never paid for their teaching efforts. Nor were physicians paid to attend who were employees of the University. The latter group had been provided a salary and assigned an academic title by the university. Teaching was not an obligation of this diverse group. They began as Instructors for one to two years, then worked their way over the years up the academic ladder. The next rung was Assistant Professor. An Assistant Professor would have to publish a minimum of eight to ten scientific papers over a six-year time frame in order to get promoted in the seventh year to Associate Professor. An Associate Professor had to carve out an area of research interest or develop clinical expertise in a single subject. He or she needed to establish a national reputation, be active on committee structures within the University and the Medical School, and participate in national organizations as well. After ascending to committee Chairpersons in local, a few regional and maybe a national office over the years, plus publishing at least 30 scientific papers, an Associate Professor could be considered for full Professorship. In the equation of Medical School Promotions Committees, teaching of medical students and residents was not valued compared to research productivity and publications. A great teacher who had not published or acquired funds from outside the university for research projects did not necessarily get promoted to full Professor. Those employed by the University who placed teaching as their own priority were admired by students. As a group, we were able to designate one physician who would win an annual Teaching Award. But the frameable certificate was more of a symbolic gesture of thanks. I and others nominated Dr. Thomas Keith.

At the time of my vote, I was a fourth year medical student (junior intern) who assumed the responsibilities of patient care, as if I had graduated from medical school with the M.D. degree. This was of course a year away, and the junior internship was meant to provide me the confidence to be a real doctor. Every three days I was placed in the position of making decisions about new admissions and on a daily basis for all patients under my care I committed orders to the nursing staff. Dr. Neilson was my guardian senior resident for the I.M. ward team. Dr. Thomas Keith was the Associate Professor of Internal

Medicine, our attending physician for a month, who volunteered his services as a teacher.

Dr. Keith came daily at the end of our working rounds. He was late on the majority of days. We would often receive a call from his wife indicating a variable length of delay. Dr. Keith would arrive breathless, neck tie knot hanging awkwardly, face half covered with blood or cotton fibers and dried stiptic remnants. His physical appearance and apparent ineptitude for chores of daily living was in contrast to his body of knowledge, which was profound. Dr. Keith's area of expertise was the evaluation and management of patients with elevated blood pressure. He was consulted regularly for his thoughts regarding hypertension from within the University, and he had been recognized nationally through his publications on the topic. His national audience did not know that he invariably left one or even two of his shoe laces untied.

I vividly remember several patient contacts under Dr. Keith's supervision. A middle-aged gentleman had an acute episode of chest pain. The man had been on the surgical floor of the hospital receiving treatment for burns. The burns were sustained while grilling out. He foolishly squirted lighter fluid on smouldering charcoals, and the flames leapt to his clothing, denuding the skin of his right arm and chest. The man had a past history of a blood clot occurring in his lung. In order for the surgeons to scrub the man's burned skin on a daily basis, they stopped the man's blood thinner. With the chest pain, he was transferred from the surgical floor to the medical floor. Dr. Neilson felt a heart attack was most likely. Dr. Keith insisted a repeat blood clot was most likely and showed us all the changes on the man's electrocardiogram (E.K.G.) that sealed the diagnosis.

A young adult with hypertension and a positive family history for early death from heart disease presented to the E.D. with chest pain following exertion. I was dispatched to the E.D. to provide his definitive care. I found an ill-appearing, ashen-colored man with profuse sweating. Indeed, he looked as if he had suffered a heart attack. Dr. Neilson suggested initiating treatment for a heart attack. Because of a subtle change on the blood gas, Dr. Keith instructed me to initiate antibiotics for pneumonia. Dr. Keith recognized the man's chest x-ray showed no changes to suggest pneumonia and there was an absence of fever, yet he insisted on the diagnosis. Within 12-24 hours the man developed cough, fever and the x-ray changes one would anticipate with pneumonia.

Ms. Rhodelia Crenshaw had eye surgery for which she was hospitalized. On the first post-operative day, she walked to her bathroom. She felt lightheaded while on the commode and depressed a wall-mounted panic button before she fainted. The nurses found Ms. Crenshaw unconscious on the floor with a heart rate of 40 beats per minute. At a physician's order, the nurses gave her a medication that sped her heart rate up to normal. They then transferred her to the medical service. Ms. Crenshaw was admitted to the I.C.U. under my care. She was maintained for three days in the I.C.U. and had no further problems. She was transferred to the usual hospital ward floor and remained without any symptoms. On working rounds, Dr. Neilson indicated Ms. Crenshaw had been the recipient of maximal hospital benefit. In his estimate, she could be discharged. I wrote the order for discharge before Dr. Keith arrived for attending rounds. At the time Dr. Keith spoke of Ms. Crenshaw on rounds, she was entering a cab in the accompaniment of her preacher. Dr. Keith suggested we stress Ms. Crenshaw by having her walk up and down the ward for a few hours on both the morning and afternoon before we sent her home tomorrow morning. My eyes met Dr. Neilson's, and neither one of us told Dr. Keith we had already sent her home. Around lunch time, I received an outside page. The woman who called me was seeking information from the treating physician. She indicated she was calling from the coroner's office. It seemed Ms. Creshaw exited the cab unassisted and fell dead beside her preacher on her front walkway. I gave the background of her hospitalization and hung up the phone. Having lost all interest in eating, I sought Dr. Neilson's counsel. On attending rounds the next day, we advised Dr. Keith of our actions. He listened intently and replied unangered, "I thought we could have kept her another day."

In autumn of the following year, when I had been conferred the M.D. degree, Dr. Keith apparently fell off a ladder while cleaning leaves from his gutter. He was hospitalized for a broken back, and his spine injury confined him for some time to a wheelchair. I decided to let a roofer clean the gutters of our newly-purchased home. I also decided I could do a better job of learning one area of medicine well, strive to apply the book knowledge to clinical encounters, and whenever possible, guide the learners of medicine with the patience exhibited by Dr. Keith.

Dr. Herb Flessa, also an internist, showed the same enthusiasm for teaching medical students. He gravitated to caring for patients with blood disorders. He seemed to dabble in other ailments of adults and had a broader perspective of internal medicine than Dr. Keith. He also delighted in playing touch football with us on Saturday afternoons. Dr. Flessa knew the nuts and bolts of common presentations with a specific disease and took note of unusual presentations. He stored the information in his data bank, and when faced with the mirror circumstance in the future made the association and shared the knowledge. As a result, he was an astute clinician. He loved the spontaneity of discussing a patient with an unknown diagnosis with students on rounds. He was less intent on publishing papers than many academic attendings, yet promoted the concept of writing as an admirable pursuit. He encouraged me as a fourth year student to submit a case report to the medical literature. He was my attending when two brothers, home on leave from the military, placed marijuana leaves in a spoon, heated them, extracted the fluid and then gave it into each other's veins. The two had not thought out the consequences of their actions. I don't think they anticipated ending up in the I.C.U. At the time of the encounter, scholarly individuals debated whether this form of drug abuse theoretically could stimulate the clotting factors involved in controlling bleeding. At Dr. Flessa's suggestion, we engaged Dr. Helen Glueck, a research physician with expertise in bleeding disorders. We proved that intravenous injection of marijuana indeed altered clotting factors. I collected appropriate background articles from the library and wrote a rough draft of a case report. Unfortunately, I left the writing project on a shelf after I completed the junior internship in medicine. Years later, someone published an article in *Journal of American Medical Association* that demonstrated what our cases had shown. This was unfortunately one of three circumstances were one of my observations, if committed to a complete manuscript and submitted, may have been accepted as new medical information.

Dr. Ron Straus also had a strong desire to publish new information. At the time we crossed paths, he was a sapling among a mature, forested community of pediatric blood specialists. Dr. Straus was an Instructor fighting to establish his identity. He was surrounded by fellow faculty who held a national reputation. Over the years, five of their ranks left to head their own departments at prestigious medical centers. Dr. Straus ultimately deserved the same opportunity to lead others. He set an example for me long before he departed Cincinnati. Dr. Straus carried a loose leaf 4x6" book in his right coat pocket. When he taught students and residents on rounds, he could quote from memory the physician's name who first wrote on the subject in question. He often knew the physician's first name and middle initial. He knew which journal printed the article and which year it was published. On rare occasion, Dr. Straus needed to double check his recall and out would come his personal encyclopedia. Rarer still, if he could not provide a reference for a topic discussed at rounds, he would appear at the next rounds with a copy of the article for all of us. Few students cherished as much as I reading copies of a 1944 case report on swelling over the breast bone due to mumps or a 1918 review of a thousand consecutive patients evaluated at the Bronx's Millard Filmore Hospital with chickenpox.

Dr. Ed Pratt bridged the past and present. When Dr. Pratt was in his youth, he worked with several pioneers in pediatric medicine. He learned from them the clinical practice of medicine and the capacity to write and edit medical articles. Now near his retirement, he was engaged in senior administrative responsibilities. To many of my student colleagues, he was a dry man who related too distant information to be of utility. For me, Dr. Pratt brought insight about early explorations made by his supervisors and added his own observations and discoveries when he made rounds. No matter how tied up he was with the department, he stopped to teach. He emphasized points with subtle, self-effacing humor. If he seemed outwardly stodgy and stiff in the hospital, I saw him play ping-pong with youthful abandon. During a faculty skit at a joyous Christmas party, he bared his chest to punctuate a joke. Contrary to any assertion otherwise, this man had heart.

A heart may have been missing from the chests of Drs. Carl Morten, Eli Chester and Wilmia Larkin. That biologic aberration may have been the reason for their lasting imprint.

When Carl Morten precepted students, they cowered at his stern demeanor. He once hosted a student party in his home, and none were brave enough to come. One of my colleagues, seeing Dr. Morten come down the hospital hallway, locked himself in a medical treatment room until Dr. Morten had passed.

Dr. Chester's rigidity on rounds was equally frightening. One case demonstrated the point. A three-year-old blonde boy named Miles Steuben had undergone an elective tonsillectomy. One week later, Miles bled from the operative site onto his angelic face, his clothing and his father's clothing. Miles came under my care when readmitted to the hospital. He remained stable without further bleeding for a day on my ward, then rebled. He was transferred to the I.C.U. when he went into shock. Miles received multiple blood transfusions. The ear, nose and throat doctors inserted packing in Miles' throat to stem the bleeding. He returned to my ward with the bulky packing being held in place by a string that hung out his mouth. He soon had the freedom of the hallways, and during our attending rounds, he walked between Dr. Chester and us. Master Steuben tugged at my leg, looked up at my face, string hanging from his mouth and said, "Hi, Dr. Singer; I feel good today," then kept walking toward the play room. All of us burst out in laughter at the bravery and innocence of this little boy. Dr. Chester was disgruntled that rounds were interrupted by something frivolous.

Dr. Larkin was impervious to anything happening out of the immediate sphere of her attending rounds. She arrived at 1 PM daily expecting us all to be present in the ward conference room, even if a patient deteriorated and needed attention. She arrived early one day and overheard a nurse approach me indicating Mary Renae Tipton's IV had infiltrated. She was on an 8 AM-2 PM-8 PM-2 AM schedule of intravenous chloramphenicol to treat her bacterial meningitis. I indicated to the nurse Mary Renae's antibiotics would be given when

I restarted the IV after rounds. Dr. Larkin overheard the conversation, turned to me and said, "You have 20 minutes to find the appropriate reference that proves the nurse can give the next dose of chloramphenicol on time by mouth rather than by a delayed intravenous route." Not having Dr. Straus available, I literally ran to the Research Library and manually poured over materials until I found the historic document. Remember, this was the pre-computer age. I hurried back to rounds which were in progress and gave my report. Dr. Larkin was satisfied that I was now aware a researcher had long ago discovered the blood levels of chloramphenicol were equal following either an oral or an intravenous dose.

Dr. Aaron Pearlman spoke softly and carried the same big stick. Dr. Pearlman devoted his orthopedic career to children. He took special interest in repairing deformities created by neurologic diseases of childhood. He surgically lengthened tendons of children with spastic cerebral palsy and placed rods in the spines of children whose back curvature impaired their quality of life. In between these cases, he tended to children who fractured bones in falls from playground equipment or evaluated the need for serial casting on children who had rotational deformities such as knock knees, toe-in gait, or bowleggedness. Dr. Pearlman taught pediatric bone diseases to orthopedic residents who rotated at the children's hospital for a three month time frame. Besides service with passion, Dr. Pearlman also gave of himself to students and residents on pediatrics. He was comfortable giving a dissertation from the podium, but appeared more at ease with small group discussion or one on one instruction. Because he was intelligent, giving, kind and gentlemanly in all ways, he participated in many hospital committees. During the group dynamics, he never took sides on an issue but listened intently to a debate. Dr. Pearlman formulated an opinion, and during the final deliberations, the Chair of a committee often turned to Dr. Pearlman for his opinion. Dr. Pearlman spoke quietly to the hushed silence about him, and a vote taken after his discussion generally favored Dr. Pearlman's solution.

Although I appreciated his diplomacy, the intensity of circumstances often directed my passion to polarize opinion. I can only claim that genuine warmth, tact and persistence was of help in one important relationship.

EVOLUTION OF A RELATIONSHIP

In 1971, the summer that separated the third from the fourth year of medical school, Ruth married me, ending multiple years of less than upbeat and optimistic enthusiasm for my mateless condition.

TWENTY-TWO

Moss-grown bole and gnarled bark
Proclaim its age and wisdom.
Sprightly in youth, it did not succumb
To the gusty winds which dispersed seed,
But raised its polished umbrage
To chide the water spider.
Now it watches the etching of the distant shore
And longs to grasp an aberrant current.
Its drooping leaves have listless motion,
And brittle now are its silvery branches.
Gone are the days of careless journey
For stagnancy is its manner.

We met again for the first time in my sophomore year of medical school as a result of my employment as a phlebotomist. I consented to drawing blood samples on hospitalized patients from 7 AM to 8 AM five days weekly for a dollar or so above minimum wage. Ruth and Joyce were medical technicians at University Hospital. They worked the 7 AM-3 PM shift. They began their day on the hospital's 7th floor. They drew samples of blood for tests that had been ordered by medical students, interns or residents. Ruth and Joyce started on odd rooms of the south wing of the medical wards, doubled back on the even side, transitioned to the medical intensive care unit then crossed the hall to the cardiac care unit. On my first day, Joyce provided me needed technical guidance. I gravitated to her instruction repeatedly in the first weeks. She was soft-spoken and confident. As half of a biracial marriage, she opened my eyes to unrecognized prejudice.

...AND LORD WE PRAYED ON SUNDAY

Within our religious neighborhood
(all unified in prejudice)
Winston's K. of C. Hall stood.
The four-walled, white-washed edifice
Had weathered Tuesday's thunder
But fell to Wednesday's ball and crane
Which sent the studs asunder.
Friday's pile of dirt was game
For all little scoundrels
Who molded pies with Thursday's rain
While minding not their mothers'.
I had to tell the city fathers
That when I passed on Saturday
One face was blacker than the others ...

At our first encounter, Ruth spoke of her resentment of the nursing staff. At 7 AM the night crew were clustered about a tape recorder providing morning report to the oncoming shift of nurses. The replacement crew had to acquire assignments and before disbursement, the phlebotomists were rudely awakening patients requesting blood-letting. Ruth found herself clothing uncovered people, escorting to the bathroom the newly-aroused with an urgency to void or establishing the correct anatomic alignment that would most likely deposit someone's elimination into a bed pan. She also maligned the doctors in training for not knowing what specimens of blood to order. She criticized the clerks for filling out the requests for blood samples incorrectly. Yet, when she contacted the patient, she was warm beyond expectation.

Ruth sensed the uneasiness I had with the unfamiliarity of

purposefully inducing pain. She noticed my visible tremor before and after the procedure and made relaxing comment about the physical sweat I produced. I was fearful of failure to acquire blood despite a stick for patients who didn't have fat, palpable, immobile veins. Only with time and encouragement of Joyce or Ruth was I able to face fragile, rolling, minuscule, seen but not felt, hidden deep, or senile varieties of veins without hyperventilating. Eventually, I could even perform the hard sticks in the neck, lower extremity or a groin, a procedural proficiency that predated my student colleagues by a year.

After an hour of labor, I returned to student life, and Joyce and Ruth withdrew to the chemistry laboratory where they analyzed blood specimens. Laborious, hand-driven analysis of samples by flame spectrophotometry was being challenged by the automated analyzers. One such device, called the SMA machine, was able to rapidly provide the results of 12 different serum parameters. Samples that had been requested on a stat basis were run before the other specimens. Stat results were available between 9 and 11 AM, whereas routine specimen results were not guaranteed until 2 or 3 PM. If Ruth felt the physician was trying his hardest to render the best patient care, she would willingly draw extra blood for a last-minute request, stamp out the forms without clerical assistance. If she felt any sense of physical attraction to a young doctor, she would place his routine patient's laboratory samples at the front of the automated run, making them available soon after the stat samples.

Although it may have first been manipulative on my part when I engaged in patient care, I daily visited the chemistry lab late morning. I developed a routine where I stopped off in the microbiology lab, checked on the germ cultures of my patients, then sought out my patients' chemistries. Ruth thought my visitation was to encounter Joyce, who seemed more impressed with my headband, ponytail-length hair and full beard. Ruth took little note when I shaved, but after incremental hair cuts and more conversation with her than Joyce, I thought Ruth processed my patients' chemistries at the first of the morning. She also consented to a date.

THE FIRST DATES

On the afternoon of our first formal coupling, Ruth drove to Walker St. She arrived in hospital white clothing, bringing an immediate sparkle to the run-down, economically depressed neighborhood that encircled my formal residence. I had taken up cohabitation with Kenny Kuresman (Goose), who owned an aging home perched precariously on a hillside overlooking downtown Cincinnati. I provided rent money for sole occupation of a bedroom, and we shared all other amenities. Every time I left for the hospital, I affixed a padlock to my bedroom door, not to keep Goose out, but to foil potential home intruders, who habitually ransacked the rehabilitated structures clustered at the affluent end of Walker St. Our front door frame was several feet from the street and up two stairs. Upon entering, a bar occupied the right wall. Straight ahead was a huge window providing a partially obstructed view of steeply descending Sycamore St. The window frame leaked cold air to such an extent that a circulating bird bath inside the living room froze during the winter months. Hugging the left wall was a staircase down to two bedrooms, a bath with a periodic faltering drain and a galley kitchen.

Since Ruth's visit was before our prolonged kitchen sink malfunctioning, I was able to utilize our modest cutlery and prepare dinner. Goose voluntarily entertained Ruth until I brought the roast chicken and potatoes up to the bar side table. The meal obviously impressed Ruth as she promptly exclaimed, "You left the eyes on the potatoes!" After consumption of the tasty but visually unappealing spuds, I hoped for no further criticisms of the second half of our date.

We left Ruth's Corvaire in front of our house, and I drove my second proudly-owned 10-year-old Plymouth down the hill into the heart of the West End. I paid "protection money" to park curbside on Dalton St. A neighborhood youngster in return did not slash the tires. We attended the last game the Redlegs played at Crosley Field. In my mind the Reds beat the Cardinals, but I'm unsure of the accuracy of that assertion. We returned to Walker St. that evening. Ruth's car was not broken into. Goose's vehicle two weeks previously had the battery stolen. He replaced it. Another was stolen. He installed a locking device on his hood. Ruth drove six miles west of our home to her apartment on Harrison Ave. Other than the potatoes, she recalls little of the day. In contrast, I shared my strange sensation with Goose. I told him I intended to marry Ruth Hoenemeyer.

Crosley Field had the capacity to alter your senses. It was one of baseball's original field of dreams. You felt on top of the players, even when seated in the outreaches of the grandstands. Only a few seats had obstructed views. Real people occupied the seats, especially the true fans in the sun deck/moon deck, which rested behind the right field wall. Even truer fans occupied the spaces beyond the left field wall. Several impromptu loggers often secured perches on a wooden electrical fixture that was in line with the foul post. Other revelers typically ascended the roof of a laundry in dead left field. At the game, you celebrated life with an affordable bag of peanuts, downed a large lemonade and threw its lid, frisbee style, hoping that it could reach the grass mowed parallel by loving curators. I first entered Crosley with my pack of Cub Scouts, found the environment fascinating and sought to return at any possible time. When the mood struck us, and we had saved or stolen (in my circumstance) sufficient money, Brother and I would seek two other adventurers. Four people could take a cab to the ball park for 50¢ a head. Alternately, in the innocent era of the 50's and 60's, you could safely reach the ballpark by bus.

The sensations I felt at night's end of our first date may have been from a flood of released nostalgia. Against my mother's insistence, I hoarded baseball cards throughout the 1950's. Five cards were packaged with a decay-promoting sheet of bubble gum. Twenty packages of five cards were available in a cigar-box-sized container that hid neatly under my underwear. The night of our first date, I had a sense that Ruth was as precious as the complete baseball cards for the entire 1956 Redlegs roster.

After several in-city dates that included a walk on the newly-laid artificial turf of the yet-to-be-opened Riverfront Coliseum and distant visits such as a picnic at Clifton Gorge near Xenia, Ohio, and the Ohio State Fair in Columbus, the joy of her presence and the intensity of my feelings persisted. Our enthusiasm for each other was sustained and uninterrupted until one party at our place. One of Goose's inebriated guests, outside my bedroom, who had shared my marijuana, swayed, lurched to a flexed position then vomited the sedatives and analgesics he had previously inhaled. Ruth turned to me and raised the question, "Is this your idea of fun?" She indicated she could not get more serious with me unless I gave up recreational marijuana use.

Pops had told me that marijuana made him sloppy, and he couldn't quantitate the degree of inebriation with pot as he could with alcohol. He indicated that if I could handle a warped time perception and temporary incoordination, he found marijuana use pharmacologically acceptable.

UPON AN INTRODUCTION TO MARY JANE

I spoke of difficult matters with the under sea lord.
A ghastly green fellow was he with the gills of enormity.
And bubbles flowing endlessly from every port.
We kept company and played among the reefs,
Alone, then joined by those who know.
Blue, indeed the sea.
How quiet was the noise;
Splashes free flowing, concentric, unseen.
Dilemma, all caused by the moon, indeed.
Customary it is to bow before him,
But I found him lacking in custom.
How natural can that be?
Surprised I was indeed.
Surname, he asked.
Self questions he proposed and answered them in rows
Inverse. Converse, oh yes, converse.
Indeed.
Such a jolly time prevailed,
I hardly noticed his tale.

I easily gave up recreational use of illicit substances. I was in love.

LOVE'S STRUGGLE

Love for me came slowly to Ruth. My efforts to spend time with her were partially hampered by being on call every three days. During the 30-hour stretches within the hospital, I rarely had an opportunity to deal with outside, real-world issues. A telephone conversation with Ruth was an infrequent luxury. As an example, when I called at sundown while sitting on the rooftop of the Veteran's Administration Hospital early autumn, it was not possible to discuss or convey my feelings toward her. She did express that it seemed romantic since fellow students Mike Sunday and Rick Sieving were sharing the twilight view with me. At many other attempted telephone calls, I made contact with Ruth's roommate, Kathy. She hid the fact that Ruth was generally out on a date with another suitor.

My competition for Ruth's love was a gainfully-employed owner of fashionable clothing who traveled about Cincinnati in a Corvette. He was a Christian, engaging spirit who had discretionary income to properly entertain a woman. I, too, sought the joys of life, but by superficial comparison, I was a somewhat off-centered fellow with only one clean sheet on the mattress who wore moth-holed underwear. The passenger side door of my Plymouth sparked like a flint stone upon door closure. I was without any source of income. I was in debt to the American Medical Association for medical school loans. Because it was given to me unsolicited in the mail, I owned a Shell gasoline credit card but was otherwise without charge cards.

With the passage of time, I was able to surmount the financial inequities between wooers. Ruth was ultimately humbled by wildflowers I picked for her. These gifts served more to promote our friendship than to magnify my noble quality of poverty. The passion of the poems I wrote about our relationship illustrated the profit of our continued association. For anyone keeping score, there were pluses in my column under intellectual capacity, intrinsic creativity and apparent motivation. However, I had a few strikes in the negative column. Two were emphasized by Kathy who saw me as a non-Christian, and even more unforgiving, an East Side inhabitant of Cincinnati. When I ultimately proposed marriage to Ruth before the other guy sought a permanent relationship with her, Ruth sought Kathy's advice. Thank God Ruth ignored Kathy's response.

THE IN-LAWS

In an exhilarated mood, Ruth and I stayed up all night and traveled near dawn to my future in-laws' home. We parked, awaited the sunrise to co-announce our intentions. Ruth, eager to please parents she loved, lacked the resilience to face their scrutiny. She requested to break the news later, by herself.

I did not see Ruth's grace under fire. I only knew my future father-in-law, Bill (Willy) was always glad to share my company on a Sunday. He celebrated my visitation with purchase and co-consumption of draft beer. As a result of my visits, on more than one occasion, Willy spent a post-visitation evening at St. Francis-St. George Hospital, receiving care for exacerbation of his congestive heart failure. Once I served him homemade chicken soup, laden with Matzo meal dumplings, he spent eight hours under the E.D.'s evaluation for abdominal pain severe enough for their strong consideration of acute appendicitis. Although his cardiovascular system was weak and his stomach lacked a Jewish detonating device, he had the strength of acceptance. He permitted me his younger daughter's hand. Throughout my association, I watched Willy daily attend early morning Mass, where his prayers remained unknown to me. But if he had doubts about the longevity or intensity of my affection for his daughter, he never showed them before me.

Future mother-in-law, "Big" Ruth, had to deal with Willy's post-visitation ailments. She was typically less happy to welcome my visits. Ruth had known of a circumstance where a monetarily-challenged medical student married a working girl, completed his training, then divorced her. I perceived that Ruth retained in her mind a lingering reservation, worried that I would abandon her daughter.

THE WEDDING

Rick Sieving had married freshman year of medical school. He suggested that the most successful tactic I could take was to passively accept any recommendations the Honemeyers made regarding the wedding. I did so. They arranged for a Mass at Bellerman Chapel on the campus of Xavier University. The evening before the event at an on-site rehearsal, we found flowers decorating the altar. They had been retained from a recent wedding. The good Father at my request was willing to keep them in place for an additional day. Since my love had paid for my wedding suit, the shoes, both of our wedding rings and her bridal bouquet, she had abandoned the expenditure of church decoration. The only episode that negated the joy of that evening was my failure to clean the inside of my car. I had washed the exterior and applied much-needed wax, but Ruth cried when her dress was soiled by contact with accumulated dirt on the interior. I rectified the situation that evening and made no other wedding-related errors that caused her to stir.

We had sent a handwritten note to a small number of friends and family to join us.

Willy attended our wedding on crutches. He had just undergone foot surgery and bore a fresh scar, hiding a screw. His flat effect on the wedding photos was the additive result of an unbearably muggy day and his post-operative pain. The screw on Mrs. Honemeyer's face and apparent discomfort was emotional. She was troubled that only the left half of the congregation took communion. She felt that my fellow medical student, Stuart Cutler, was a poor substitute for a professional photographer.

The immediate family of adults consumed a substantial luncheon at the Vernon Manor, a historic hotel that brought elegance to an enconomically depressed center of Cincinnati. A few hours later, Ruth's family receded. My family and our friends assembled at the baseball diamond in Eden Park for the official reception.

Ruth and I had expected our contemporaries to enjoy the day, and I think they did. To our surprise, the old folks in attendance were exhilarated. Cousin Winkler, a driven business man who was only a few years from his first heart attack, frolicked carefree in the outfield. Pop's brother, Joe, who had unexpectedly accepted our invitation and traveled from Chicago, played infield with the ease of an adolescent.

THE HONEYMOON

My Plymouth, no matter how temporarily spiffy, could not be trusted for a lengthy trip. The steering wheel of Ruth's Corvair routinely shook violently. Making things worse, the interior of the trunk accumulated rainwater, placing uneven and shifting weight over the front wheels. We opted to rent a full-size car for the honeymoon trip to Canada.

We consumed a tank of 29¢-a-gallon gasoline by the time we reached our first planned destination, Stratford, Ontario. The little town had acheived acclaim for its Shakespearian theater. Apparently folks came from far and wide for the plays, but no one must have stayed over night. None of the hotel chains were located within the region. Months in advance of our arrival, I booked Mr. Majors' Hotel. The description in the AAA book was sparse, but the two stars made it a cut above the others listed.

Mr. Majors greeted us in the centrally-located office, determined that we were honeymooners and assigned the room farthest from the sparsely-traveled country road. Ruth found the accommodations acceptable with the exception of a maroon toilet seat. She didn't trust the implied cleanliness of the paper bib. She forced me to sit down before she would grace its seat. Upon returning after a play and dinner, we found no other cars in the parking lot. All was quiet until predawn when cows were let out on to the adjacent field. At 6 AM a freight train rumbled by within a stone's throw of our back wall. The engineer repeatedly sounded warning horns before a potential encounter with an auto at the non-gated crossing. The story repeated itself the following day.

Sleep deprived, we explored the town's shops and bought an old wooden chest that was encrusted with paint. The chest fit snugly on its side in the rear of the car. It didn't budge during our later time in Toronto or brief stay on the Canadian side of Niagra Falls. When we declared the purchase at the border, the officer had us disassemble every rectangle as he searched for contraband. I guess he felt it was not natural for us to purchase furniture when the nature of our visit had been to honeymoon. I was less disturbed than Ruth, for this had been my second honeymoon encounter with an officer of the law.

Medical student-photographer Stuart Cutler had lived with Anita for quite a few years. Their wedding ceremony, planned when the moment felt right, took place inside the ornamental trolley car of Devou Park in Covington, Ky. They invited me afterwards to attend their honeymoon. They journeyed first to Pittsburgh. A mentally retarded adult possessed a more complete series than Stuart of all the functioning trolleys in the United States. I entertained Anita while Stuart perched on a traffic island patiently waiting for a white trolley. His photo completed his Pittsburgh series. We meandered east, ultimately settling in New Hampshire. We enjoyed the late August air for a week. On returning home, we got caught in a thick midnight fog. We pulled off the road and slept. I awoke to the stirrings of a state trooper, who was on the opposite end of a very strong flashlight. He projected the flood light into the rear seat, across my face, onto the tent to my right, then on to Anita in the passenger seat. The officer surveyed Stuart and asked, "What are you doing here?"

Stuart replied, "The fog caught us by surprise, so we stopped, planning to continue when it cleared."

"Where have you come from?"

"The White Mountains of New Hampshire," he said.

"Where are you going?"

"Cincinnati."

"What have you been doing?"

Stuart said, "We have been on our honeymoon."

I felt my brain scream as the officer's light rapidly rotated among our three faces, again and again as he contemplated whether to arrest us. The officer let us go after considering the illogical nature of our circumstance. We returned home safely. Stuart and Anita returned to their apartment which was within a mile of us. They shared the apartment with Stuart's turtles, named Dartos and Detrusor, after muscle planes in the human male groin.

OUR ABODE

The night of our wedding, I lost my virginity in the temporary bedroom of our narrow row home we shared from a few months before the wedding until a few months after our first wedding anniversary.

Mr. and Mrs. Carter had purchased the circa-1900 building as an investment. They rented the first floor to a free-spirited couple in their early 20s. We occupied the second floor, which was accessible by a side entrance. The kitchen, with a 25-year-old gas stove that served in cold weather as a source of heat for the bathroom, was to the right of the staircase. To the left were two small rooms. The furthest faced the street. Its windows opened onto the porch roof, Ruth's infamous projected escape route. We eventually rehabilitated a lightless, heatless, six-foot-tall attic and with materials purchased by Mr. Carter, fashioned the eventual bedroom and study. Mr. Carter, pleased that we improved his investment, purchased for us a rug and returned $10/month for weekly taking in the garbage cans and tending to the small yard.

In the center of the back yard, we uprooted rocks and planted flowers and any vegetables that had the audacity to survive. Unknown to Ruth, the couple downstairs planted marijuana. The occasional smell of their burning harvest drifted up our forced air ducts. The fumes were more palatable than the dog excrement which was a constant from their golden retriever, housed in the basement. The first time marijuana penetrated the second floor, Ruth declared, "They are cooking with Indian spices." She had associated the smell with a previous neighbor's apartment during her freshman year at University of Cincinnati. I informed her that our neighbors were smoking grass and obviously the Indian graduate student next to her in her Clifton apartment had smoked dope as well.

OTHER REVELATIONS

Ruth found it different rooming with me compared to her previous female mates. In contrast to their behaviors, I left used but clean clothing thrown accessibly over chairs for reuse and placed soiled dishes in a heap, pending a collective cleansing. I left Kleenex tissues in the pants pockets of clothes about to be washed. I did not separate my whites. Ruth was occasionally vocal about these acts and other expressions of masculinity.

On the other hand, I was unprepared to see a woman enter a bedroom wearing hair curlers. Whereas I retired in briefs, Ruth wore a red pajama top, matching ¾-length pajama bottoms and high-top, brown woolen socks. I took refuge under a blanket; she preferred no covers. Our differences were frictional until she farted one night under the sheets.

We were comfortable companions until I sought to open a charge account at Sears. We were contemplating the purchase of a window air conditioner. I told Ruth I would like to acquire my first legitimate charge card. She was leery but by my side when I provided the customer agent my demographics. When he learned I had no prior credit, no immediate source of income, and had outstanding loans, he lifted his head from his data sheet. He looked at me straight in the eye and repeated the information in a tone of disbelief. Ruth announced she was going to the rug department and left. The customer agent said to his supervisor, "Hey Rick, come here and hear this!" The two of them gave me a card based on Ruth's income and advised me not to divulge our conspiracy.

Money, or more appropriately the lack of money, was not a distraction for the first year of our marriage. The distraction was the time apart during my fourth year of medical school. I had been accustomed to my intermittent in-hospital imprisonment and didn't realize how unnatural my life was until a Friday evening while on-call. I made four unsuccessful efforts to reach Ruth by phone to be sure she was prepared for an evening of solitude. When I received no answer, a fellow student covered for me, and in a state of panic I drove home. I negotiated a desolated "Pill Hill," Cincinnati's collection of hospitals, and passed through the bar scene adjacent to the University. I found

Ruth comfortably immersed in the tub with a novel. She had been unable and unwilling to answer the telephone. On my return to the hospital, I envied the revelers teaming in the streets, unaware of stress. These people were also planning to stay up all night, but I projected their sleep deprivation was more idyllic.

OTHER FOURTH-YEAR STRESSORS

When brother and I were in elementary school, Grandpa Rukin rode the 47 Route bus with us. He exited in South Avondale, within walking distance of his pinocle games. Our destination was the downtown Y.M.C.A. where we spent the day. If Mom's packed lunch was deemed insufficient, we would cross Central Parkway's median strip for Frisch's Restaurant. If you gracefully held the door open for all entering or exiting customers during their lunch peak, you would often receive enough change to purchase a Big Boy. After one such successful pilgrimage, on our return to the Y.M.C.A. a man as bald as Grandpa was awkwardly postured on one of the benches. As we neared, it was obvious that he was pale and frozen in this partial slump. I noted on closer inspection he did not flinch when a fly flew into his right nostril. I asked Barry what this all meant. As the siren of an approaching ambulance wailed, Barry explained that the man had died. I had no concept of death, but decided on the spot that the state held no attraction, and the vocalizations of the transport vehicle signaled an adverse outcome.

In my fourth year of medical school, an ambulance brought a child who had swallowed two or three of her mother's Lomotil tablets twelve hours previously. The mother thought the child's ingestion of an extra pill or two above what the mother had been prescribed for her diarrheal illness would not be a concern. In the morning, the mother found the child seizing. The narcotic medication within Lomotil had depressed her child's drive to breathe. The child suffered irreversible brain damage from the lack of oxygen. The child's seizures, reflecting the brain insult, continued until her death, despite my provision of all available anticonvulsant medications and supportive care.

Ambulances carried passengers of a vehicle that had lost its brakes on one of Cincinnati's most steeply inclining roads, Ravine St. The adults were extracted from the almost unrecognizable van and transported to University Hospital. Two children, both in extremis, were brought to us at Children's Hospital Medical Center. One child survived briefly in the I.C.U., but the brother died before me in the Emergency Department.

During my 4th year, I relived these and other deaths. Screams of the mother who lost her child from heart disease uncontrollably reverberated from our bedroom walls. I saw the ghost of Mr. Ballor walk up Stratford Ave. He chatted with a nurse across our street and they both listened to Carley Simon's "You're So Vain." That song echoed through her window over and over at a volume that could wake the dead. With time, the visions and sounds haunted me less, but the acquisition of a diploma at year's end did not signal a new journey without stress.

THE GRADUATION

The administrative dignitaries in the Dean's office at the University of Cincinnati College of Medicine plus the professors gathered stage left and we, the students, huddled alphabetically stage right. Our spouses, parents, and friends assembled in the audience to witness the graduation ceremony. From the audience pit, trumpets blared, flags waved in the aisles and a symbolic monument was raised for our perseverance and accomplishments.

INVOCATION

While students, their advisors spoke approving,
Cheering words and held over each a triumphal arch.
Promising letters of recommendations were gladsome and soothing.
Harmonious interviews spirited and captured hearts.
These were the apt, endowed, serene

Whose Honors–stenciled transcripts attested
To academic worth as governing routine.
They'd sown seeds of felicity and were people-directed.
We were blessed to have gained their match.
Now, prophecy over time fulfilled, tonight, they frolic.
We've gathered to pray that a monument be raised,
Perhaps engraved in golden letters and set aloft
That summons remembrance of our consensual praise.
This congratulatory moment needs sublime extension.

Reprinted from *Academic Emergency Medicine* 1:120, 1994.

A learned physician had traveled from his distant academic institution in order to impart a graduation message. The Dean introduced the dignitary, "I'm pleased to introduce you to our guest speaker, who completed his medical degree at the University of North Carolina College of Medicine. He trained in Internal Medicine at John's Hopkins School of Medicine. He completed a fellowship in Infectious Disease at Emory University. He joined the faculty as an Assistant Professor at Duke Medical Center, ascended to Associate Professor at the University of Tennessee School of Medicine. He became full professor while at the University of Kentucky School of Medicine. He took a sabbatical to work at the Center for Disease Control in Atlanta before joining the faculty at Georgetown University. The Dean was less than half the way through our speaker's career when my father blurted, "Guess he couldn't hold down a job!" The entire auditorium heard Pop's remark, and a few acknowledged his irreverence with a giggle.

All but three students who were present at our convocation four years earlier were participants in the graduation exercise.

IN THEIR NEW ACADEMIC VILLAGE

With our backs to the Sandridge formation
Viewing nameless vistas to the northwest,
We ask for You to bestow confirmation

And guidance to our newest pool of graduates.
Please give them requisite faith in themselves.
Help them find bountiful pleasure in servitude.
Let them reduce the fears of those they touch.
In the expectation of symbolic gratitude
Let them long recount stories of us.

Our diplomas were conferred by the Board of Directors of the University of Cincinnati at the recommendation of the College of Medicine faculty. The diploma signified completion of the school's structured studies. The signatures of the Dean, President of the University and the Chairman of the Board of Directors provided us with all the rights and privileges of the degree of Doctor of Medicine. In truth, without passage of the certifying exam of the State Medical Board that followed, the medical degree only gave you permission to engage in an internship.

OPPORTUNITIES WITHIN INTERNSHIP, RESIDENCY

SEEKING AN INTERNSHIP

I decided to pursue a career in pediatrics. Of the 20,000 graduates of United States medical schools in 1972, three to four thousand others gravitated to pediatrics. There were close to 100 places that offered medical school graduates three years of training in pediatrics. No more than two dozen were considered highly competitive training sites. I felt I was competitive for several institutions that had a reputation for excellence. Ruth requested that I send applications to programs in Lexington, Louisville, Cincinnati, Ann Arbor, Pittsburgh, Philadelphia and Rochester.

As a student seeking a competitive residency, you were up against 300-400 graduates vying for the same position. The reputation of your medical school spoke for itself. Your transcript provided objective data regarding your stature compared to your classmates. You sought letters of recommendations from professors, who were more likely to have a national reputation. You gave up your right to see these letters as well as the narrative constructed by your academic advisor. This letter, called the Dean's Note, detailed everyone's perception of your impact at the school during four years of book study and clinical practice. Last and most important, you had to construct a lengthy personal reflection regarding your speciality choice.

Your completed file and the academic life it represented were provided at your request to the various Program Directors. They screened your application. For the six to ten openings at each institution, each Director invited 60-80 candidates to interview. I passed the screening process and was invited to interview in all locales.

The day Ruth and I visited Rochester, it was overcast and cold. The residents took call every 48 hours, the only place in the country to retain this brutal on-call schedule. In order to support their spouses, the residents rented several homes and shared both cooking duty and house cleaning. I could not see Ruth and I more closely enduring "Indian cooking," which I feared would take place. The clincher was encountering a chicken pot pie at the Children's Hospital that was not edible. I ranked Rochester as my fourth choice.

Ruth and I enjoyed the college town atmosphere of Ann Arbor. They were my third choice since half of the training necessitated staffing a decrepit hospital in a deteriorating section of Detroit.

The Monday morning stop in Pittsburgh introduced me to Dr. Thomas K. Oliver, the most vibrant educator I had ever encountered. Awaiting my formal interview, I was instructed to sit at Dr. Oliver's side in a sequestered nook of their Children's Hospital. To his learning altar he assembled the residents who had taken call over the weekend to discuss their admitted patients. In attentive silence, I watched Dr. Oliver tangibly support the residents' judgement. He responded to relevant and critical information from the residents' presentations. He helped them capitalize on a cluster of signs and symptoms to broaden their differential diagnosis. He brought disparate clinical challenges to life. He illuminated with statesmanship, intelligence, and humor. He was principled, refined, polite beyond belief, and arrestingly luminous in his insight regarding clinical medicine. Unfortunately, their Children's Hospital was falling apart. Patient care rooms had bare lightbulbs on the ceiling. Because their planned reconstruction project would not positively impact me until the very end of my training, Pittsburgh was my second choice.

Cincinnati offered every third night call except for the newborn nursery and pediatric surgery months which were every other night call. They had newly completed a four-floor clinical tower and were sequentially updating older patient care wings. Cincinnati Children's Hospital Medical Center was my first choice.

As with all other 4th year medical students, I submitted my list. The Program Directors submitted their list of preferred candidates. A computerized program matched the top choices of the student and the Program Director. Both students and institutions learned of their future on a date in the early spring referred to as Match Day. On Match Day, I was officially informed I could continue to consume Graeter's ice cream and Cincinnati-style chili.

FELLOW INTERNS AT C.H.M.C.

On July 1st I met the other medical students who matched at Children's Hospital Medical Center (C.H.M.C.) for their internship. All interns rotated on a monthly basis through the various inpatient and outpatient services within the hospital. By year's end we had shared a month or two with each other. Our intern group in our Program Director's estimate was strong in knowledge base and overpowering in our character.

OUR UNHAMPERED BRETHREN

Those with collegial spirit and regalia
Preserved in the amber of our graduations
Have long dissolved the thick of tangle
That held them to our city and the institution.
Like you, they were uprooted and transplanted
Beside the irrigation trough of an EM masthead
And held under the grow light of clinically heralded.
In truth, your predecessors were intricate threads
Of overlapping cliques occasionally held in obedience.
Once liberated from the illusion of uniformity
Their vines bore fruits in all the seasons.
Tonight, release those strands that artificially tie.

Reprinted with permission from Academic Emergency Medicine 4:602, 1997.

In July, I was randomly placed with fellow interns Bob Wells and

Mike Mellon. Wells was an angular fellow from Indiana with rough edges in the interpersonal category. But with time, we clicked. Two years later I was the best man at his wedding.

Mellon was a fast-talking, greasy-headed, grease-loving (cheese steak), light-hearted soul who was an insufferable hockey fan of the Philadelphia Flyers. He excelled at baseball and movie trivia. He was quick with a natural humor and implemented practical jokes at any opportunity.

INVOCATION

Amidst this gathering of E.M. folk and family
We pause from lifelong learning to be wise,
To express our faith and confess our vanities.
We beseech You nod sagely tonight and supply
A boast of heraldry and lasting sense of pleasure
For a group unhampered by character or timidity.
None's masqueraded 'hind the face of yesteryear–
Nor aggrandized the success of prudent felicity.
No matter how disparate their ancestral tree, they've worked
To capacity and performed the labors as they were capable.
Each expended effort in correcting faults and quirks;
All have emblazoned high tides on our calendar of mirth.

Joel Baskoff was the brightest of the group, obsessive in his detail for patient care. He knew the correct way to treat any condition and was equally opinionated in non-medical matters. When a flawed process equally divided the total number of admitted patients between Joel's ward service and my ward service, but I ended up with a far superior educational mix, he voiced his displeasure to everyone. He ultimately forced the administration to change the admissions process by threatening to resign. In his East Coast character, he was correct, but created some ill will.

Dave Jubelerier, a fair-skinned, flaming redhead from Wisconsin, also had the capacity to sporadically fly off the handle. However, he was cautiously politic and worked from within the organization to implement change. He was a dependably astute clinician and a gifted teacher.

The young features of Chicagoan Jerry Nassenbeny's choir boy face were hidden by a flowing beard. The chestnut growth greyed prematurely. He could easily have substituted—but didn't—as a store Santa. He aimed to please, and his infectious, deep laugh was only temporarily silenced by a severe case of whooping cough he contracted. Jerry, too, was an excellent teacher. His most poignant presentation was the history of his own illness. He gave this instruction at the hospital's Grand Rounds, a formal hour of weekly teaching before the entire hospital staff.

Santa could have also been played by Ross Williams. He would not have needed a pillow under the suit; he possessed a natural padding. Ross and his fellow intern John Schowinsky (ultimately his partner in private practice in a northeastern Ohio community) were both salt of the earth types. Ross was a staunch patient advocate. When over half of our class wanted to close down an emergency facility at midnight due to under utilization between 11 PM and 6 AM, Ross championed patient care needs over our own comfort. John was equally considerate. Once he called my sleeping room during internship at 4:30 AM. He apologized that he could not restart an IV on one of my patients. He knew I was asleep, and since he was up he had tried, but was unsuccessful. His effort that night was not a random act of kindness.

When on a different ward service, but sharing an on-call night with David Namerow, you were guaranteed a call. His survivalist New York/ New Jersey cerebral function was superior. He was simply procedurally challenged and frequently borrowed your manual talents.

There was a discordance between the capabilities and the actions of Arturo Thomas. He was highly intelligent but harbored knowledge lacunae. He did not understand certain medical conditions and held polarizing opinions. One example was asthma. Arturo would permit a child to wheeze incessantly without delivering standard breathing therapies because Arturo felt an asthma attack was a psychological problem. On the other hand, he favored improving medical knowledge by acquiring a biopsy of a brain on a neurologically impaired child hospitalized for comfort care near the time of imminent death.

We didn't always know the thoughts of Kikuo Itaca. He too was obviously bright and immensely knowledgeable, particularly in childhood diseases of the kidney. He was native to Japan and had spent little time in the United States before his internship. With the passage of time, he improved his communication skills but remained soft-spoken and reflective. Unlike us, he never sought a prized position in the residents' lounge for viewing a televised athletic event during a Saturday or Sunday on-call day.

Frank Greer was pleasantly eccentric. Son of an Air Force career officer, Frank was somehow caught in a neonatal time warp. Frank was convinced his professional life was to care for newborns who had sustained various tragedies and required admission to a N.I.C.U. His personal life paralleled his professional. He collected antique feeding bottles from all regions of the world.

INVOCATION

We acknowledge that life emits a fragrance and a tune
And in a way not dissimilar from our forbearers,
We give thanks tonight for life and fortune
You have lent the graduates for all these years.
Three summers ago they were discordant melodies
With roots in different soils and orchestras
That tapped both symphonic and jamboree.
But now they celebrate in harmony.
Their music's a singular delight;
A soothing sound both beauteous and bright.
The budding compassion they trumpeted and blared
Is a prelude to the composition for life they will share:
"Though their cords will be distant harp-strings,
Roomies and work mates sing forever in key."

FRIGHTFUL FIRST HOURS

At noon of July 1st, our senior resident oriented us to the ward service. He assigned Wells and Mellon ten patients each, and I was given the four remaining patients. The disparity made sense. On average there were 34 admissions daily to the hospital. Four physicians were on-call each day throughout the hospital. If the admissions were equally distributed among us, I would receive at least eight new patients over the next 20 hours.

Mellon read the charts of his patients, interviewed parents if they were at bedside, spoke with the nurses regarding a patient's status. He then examined each of the children. He recorded factual information and his interpretation of events plus his treatment plan in each of the patient's charts. This is referred to as a progress note. As interns, we discussed our thoughts on working rounds with the senior resident. We also tried to interact with the patient's attending physician. As a rule, most attending physicians made their hospital rounds each morning. They too would enter a briefer progress note, referred to as an attending note. After a discussion with the senior and various attending physicians of the patients he was assigned, Mike wrote specific directions in the order book for the nursing staff to carry out.

Throughout the hospital, the same events occurred on each of the wards. At the beginning of each month, or Change of Service Day when we all rotated to different areas of the hospital, the process was laborious and detailed. After we were familiar with our patients, rounds, decision-making and order-writing were more easily accomplished.

Wells completed his task by 5:30 PM and "signed-out" to me. That is, he told me about each of his patients. When he left them to my overnight care, I knew who required laboratory draws, x-rays, breathing treatment and the like. He specifically conveyed who I needed to reassess and what time I needed to provide those patients my attention. By what Wells transmitted, I knew he had a grasp for bedside medicine and possessed pride in his performance.

To my surprise, Mellon signed out by 3:30 PM. I wondered if anyone with lofty standards could command this new challenge with such speed. Without verbalizing any concerns, I recorded his directions regarding his patients on my log of needed actions. I bid him adieu until 7 AM.

Within a short time frame, I learned Mellon was fully conversant with a broad sweep of medical conditions, could ferret out problems and expeditiously care for all his patients. Not only were patients the benefit of his wisdom, but I profited maximally from my experiences with him. He sustained my delight for learning, enhanced my execution of our collective patient care and made the long hours in the hospital pleasurable.

Mellon's early departure that first day I eventually learned resulted from shock. Early afternoon while taking a textbook to his locker, Mike entered an enclosed space of the hallway and confronted a scene that over powered his senses. A senior resident, who had completed his three years of training at C.H.M.C. two hours earlier, was entangled with a Professor of Pediatrics. The resident was physically and verbally assaulting an elder with a national reputation. Mike had been at various arenas with gloves-off, high-stick assaults that were tamer than this exchange of non-hockey professionals. Following this uplifting observation, Mike wondered if all the residents he was now paired with were capable of expressing such a deep and enduring debt. He went home to pray.

PRAYER FOR OUR STEW

In good spirits and temper
We are gathered together
Under your embracing love.
Help bear close to our hearts
The wishes for life's bounty
Of those who's fortunes are low.
Amongst our laughter and good cheer
May it not seem forward or rude
If we ask potatoes be sweet in our stew.

Ten patients were admitted from my service from noon of July 1st until 8 AM of July 2nd. The infirm and accompanying parents came in waves. I was able to bring relief to them all. I took care of the specifics on the other patients requested by Mellon and Wells. I took no note of any other patients on the ward unless a nurse brought some concern to my attention. I survived the night without sleep.

Our senior resident led rounds at 8 AM. We rotated clockwise from the left corner of the ward. All was well until we stopped across from the nurse's station where six of the sickest patients were housed. We gathered before a child strapped in bed who was in obvious respiratory distress and receiving an intravenous drip. None of the interns knew who the patient was. The senior pulled out the assignment sheet he used the day before to divide the patients. The asthmatic child had been admitted at 10 AM July 1st, seen by the intern who wrote 24 hour orders before he departed at noon for another service. The patient had been assigned to me and I had overlooked him. The senior resident expressed his disgust with my inadequate performance. With such a salutary encouragement of medical companionship, I too wanted to go home to pray.

INPATIENT PEDIATRICS

Ninety-five to ninety-eight percent of the total patients in a pediatric practice are at any given time managed by the pediatrician in the office setting. Two to five percent of pediatric patients on any given day may unexpectedly require an evaluation in an Emergency Department. Of the patients requiring such urgent care, less than ten percent of the total seen on a daily basis in the Emergency Department are admitted to the hospital. Despite the infrequent need for a child to require inpatient care, the time-honored residency routine for properly training a pediatrician has been to strongly emphasize mastery of scientific fundamentals of in-patient care. The exacting demands of frequent, continuing interaction with sick children under the supervision of our resident teachers and tutelage of practicing physicians has been the gold standard for pediatric education.

While engaged in my training, I perceived that much of the cherished activities of inpatient care were in fact critical for my intellectual and practical ascension toward competency. I did not examine the process of my education, but as a product of this experience, my recall for inpatients has been centered on uncommon events.

Christopher Wilson was a four-year-old front seat passenger in an automobile that was struck at a high rate of speed. He was thrown head-on into the windshield and instantly broke his neck. His spinal cord was severed and the shock temporarily stopped Chris from breathing. As fate arranged events, Dr. Ron Levin, a first-year pediatric resident, and the internist, Herb Flessa, witnessed the accident and responded. They carried on mouth-to-mouth resuscitation, and when a summoned life squad arrived, placed a plastic tube in Chris's windpipe to maintain his exchange of air. Chris's spinal column was surgically fused, and he eventually recovered his capacity to spontaneously breathe. Months into his slow recovery and rehabilitation, Chris's vital signs for no apparent reason would vary wildly. Late one afternoon, while I was on an adjacent floor, Chris stopped breathing and his heartbeat was imperceptible. Due to my foot speed, I was the first resident to reach his bedside following an over-head alarm ("a code") initiated by the nursing staff. Finding him clinically dead, I beat his chest with my fist, massaged his heart while the nurse assisted his breathing. I climbed onto his bed and pumped for everything I was worth. His heart responded and he awoke, confused that I was astride him. He was transferred a month later to the hospital's Convalescent Pavilion, a hospital floor that was accessible to the main hospital underground by tunnel. Chris had a duplicate event. A minute or so after the code was sounded, I bounded past intern John Buchino through the tunnel. I repeated my successful actions on Chris, and he came around after agonizing moments. I told his mother that he might question why I kept riding him like a jockey.

On the other hand, I pulled a similarly perched I.C.U. nurse off the chest of another tragic case. A 3-year-old youngster with incapacitating headaches underwent diagnostic investigation that revealed a large brain tumor. The tumor was precariously situated in the lower portions of his brain adjacent to the centers that regulated breathing, heart rate and blood pressure. Steroid medications were initiated in order to decrease swelling about the tumor, and he electively underwent a surgical procedure three days after the diagnosis was made. He clinically died several times during the operative procedure and post-operatively. He was resuscitated but never regained consciousness. He lingered in a persistent vegetative state with a vacant stare. Without blinking, his eyes dried. Artificial tears were insufficient. He had his eyelids sewn shut. For months he lay immobile and speechless in the far corner of the Intensive Care Unit, never regaining his former life. While running the Intensive Care Unit, I was present when he quit breathing and his heart stopped. Colleen began the resuscitation, and I interrupted her efforts. We had no discussion of our ethical duties or our moral requirements. In a silent social contract, we prepared his body for viewing and ourselves for the death notification of the family.

I also pulled the young teeth of Mary Renae Tipton and her attached diminutive body off the left breast of a nurse. Mary Renae had been admitted from the Emergency Department in bad shape on my call day. She had been sick with cold symptoms for several days, then developed a higher fever at night. The following morning she refused to eat. She became less interactive with her environment throughout the day. By evening, she was unresponsive so her mother brought her in for evaluation. Meningitis was diagnosed following a lumbar puncture in the E.D. The germ *Haemophilus influenzae* had grown in the back of her nose and throat during her cold. Then the germ invaded her bloodstream. Mary Renae's own immune system was not capable of fighting off the bloodstream infection. The germs multiplied, reaching a critical level, then crossed a natural barrier into her brain.

I found Mary Renae responsive by withdrawal to any painful stimulus and she moaned incomprehensibly. She stabilized over my post-call day. The next day, my short-call day brought me no new patients. Late afternoon I asked Mary Renae's nurse, Lisa, to help me perform another lumbar puncture to be sure the germ was being eradicated from the cerebrospinal fluid by the intravenous antibiotics. Lisa placed Mary on her side, held Mary's neck and feet, curling her into a ball, thrusting her lower back toward my needle. I placed the needle into her spinal canal and filled three tubes with the spinal fluid. Mary awakened before I withdrew the needle, and she found herself in a compromised position. She opened her 3½-year-old jaws and clamped down as hard as she could on Lisa's dependent breast.

The ward's other nurses came running to uncover the cause of Lisa's blood-curdling screams. Lisa lost no skin, but was left quite bruised. My loss was based on my failure to write a manuscript concerning Mary Renae and her brother, Christopher. The day after Mary Renae's lumbar puncture, Christopher was admitted on my on-call day. He had an infection in his bloodstream from *Haemophilus influenzae*, and the germ multiplied on the soft tissues of his face. His purple-cheeked condition, called buccal cellulitis, was not unusual. However, at the time, there were no reports in the medical literature of serious infections from *Haemophilus influenzae* occurring concurrently in the same family. The state of co-invasive serious bacterial infection from *Haemophilus influenzae* was reported several years later.

Neither the nursing staff nor I were the recipients of a bite in the following encounter. Two brothers had been playing in the kitchen. Their mother, a long-standing diabetic, for no apparent reason injected her two children with several types of her insulin. In an unbalanced state, she fled the home. Several hours later the father came home from work and was told by the oldest son, "Mom bit us with her needle." He raced the boys to the E.D. The four-year-old repeated his assertion and pointed to the needle mark sites on his own thigh and his two-year-old brother's thigh. Even with our 24 hour provision of exceedingly high intravenous infusions of sugar, both boys' blood sugars still dropped significantly while they were hospitalized.

AMBULATORY CARE

The pediatric intern's exposure to patients was largely to hospitalized individuals. In the second and third (residency) years of training, there was more frequent exposure to patients in an out-patient (ambulatory) setting. Over the residency, we saw our hospitalized patients in the hospital clinic after discharge for follow-up care if the family lacked a source for longitudinal care. In the second year residents spent time alongside attending physicians in the hospital's general medical clinic. We learned through preceptorship and experience how to deal with the healthy child. We learned how to be a "primary care doctor" who assured continuity of care and enacted preventive health strategies. During my residency, I joined other physicians who explored a legislative route to protecting Ohio's children. I participated in the creation of a child restraining device legislation that mandated use of automotive restraining devices. In a general medical clinic we were precepted by pediatricians who helped promote our knowledge of normal nutrition and early childhood development. For the childless residents, the exposure to different scenarios and parental inquiries were key. I had seen children at play in our neighborhoods, was exposed to infants and young children of my colleagues, but I was clueless as to the potential within children at various ages. I learned through repeated encounters that normal kids were capable of anything. With an exploring nature and developing motor connections, trouble and toddlers were synonymous.

Young children placed non-food items in their mouths at a rate of three times per hour. On occasion, barrettes, jacks, cuff-links, rings and coins disappeared into a mouth and were swallowed. Kids placed buttons, batteries, silly putty or styrofoam in their noses, ears or vagina. They were fully capable of self-harm from any number of household appliances. They could scald themselves with hot water. They were capable of drowning in a tub if parents let their guard down only momentarily to answer a phone or doorbell. Even if children were supervised carefully, they could still submerge themselves in toilets or five-gallon buckets containing cleaning solution. They could fall from interior heights, off railings, bound through second-story screens, and outside fly off jungle gyms, slides and monkey bars. I saw these potentially disastrous, normal behaviors with frequency in the ambulatory care setting.

We were also exposed to children who were compromised from a birth injury or an acquired, chronic disease state. In various pediatric subspecialty clinics, we learned the art of "special needs" patient care. Repeatedly, I was inspired by children who persevered despite what adults labeled as a handicap. I saw children born without an arm, or lacking fingers, or having a singular, dwarfed lower extremity achieve motor milestones that you would reflexively deny as a possibility. You learned the hearing impaired were deaf, not dumb. You saw a 5-year-old with juvenile diabetes inject himself with insulin as if the process were part of a normal kindergartner's experience. You met children who were born with a three-chambered heart, creating a physiologic state resembling a frog's, and they bounded with life. One such young man from Bloomington, Indiana lives forever in my heart.

When I first met the four-year-old lad with a complex heart condition, he was stunted in height. His lips were chronically purple since birth from blood containing lower levels of oxygen circulating in his system. He was hospitalized due to greater fatigue. I interviewed his parents the night before he underwent a catherization of his heart. The family traveled several hours from their home, and the mom was also fatigued. She was visibly pleased by my non-medical inquiries about life in a college town.

The following evening the family headed back home. It was over a year later while awaiting arrival of an elevator that I caught sight of the mom and child approaching from the hospital's front entrance. With the two hand in hand, not ten feet away, I asked, "Hey, Bloomington, how are you guys doing?"

Mother released her grip, placed her open palm at the back of his neck, and pushed him forward while responding, "Josh, tell the doctor how you are doing." I bent at the waist to hear his angelic response, and he drove his right-angled boot tip into my left shin.

I nearly crumbled, and answered, "It seems he is doing fine."

The elevator opened and I hobbled in. The doors closed me into an isolation chamber. To this day, I suspect they may have unfortunately heard a muffled trail of my uncomplimentary soliloquy regarding Hoosiers.

MILIEU OF THE EMERGENCY DEPARTMENT

We spent four to six months over a three-year time frame staffing the pediatric emergency departments at the University Hospital or at C.H.M.C. The emergency department's provided a bridge between primary care and specialty services. The emergency departments offered the attractive elements of both disciplines, while maintaining a unique position of 24 hour accessibility for care. In this interface between in-hospital and ambulatory care, I found my nitch.

INVOCATION

We rejoice that your embrace shepherds our deeds
As we respond to those whose vital signs evoke
The controlled panic of a prehospital stampede.
We're appreciative that you've spared the death stroke
For singular patrons who've attempted a discharge
From tri-monogrammed A's of DK, CV, MV, or AA.
Each of our graduates has had their database enlarged;
The aggregate will weather the Board's ultimate assay.
You cajoled a minority to a preeminent scale.
We're conscious that you sustained the cures
Of those who willed that common good prevail.
And, gathered tonight, we beseech their effectiveness endures.

Reprinted with permission from *Academic Emergency Medicine* 2:119,1995.

ADDRESSING CHIEF COMPLAINTS

The historian was the person who voiced their main concern or complaint of the patient. In some cases the child was the historian, but more often the accompanying parent was the dominant presenter of the chief complaint. Sometimes the concern was easily expressed. "He fell through the floor board and I saw him in the middle of the roadway."

In this case, the unrestrained 2-year-old collapsed the cardboard that had until then protected family members from falling through the rusted-out floor board. In the reflection of her rear view mirror, the mother saw the child tumbling uncontrollably on southbound I-75. The toddler miraculously was not struck by traffic that followed in the far right lane. After he was transported to the E.D. we determined he had fractured his pelvis and left femur. The displaced bones had blocked the blood supply to a now very purple leg. We recruited the necessary physicians with the surgical skills to repair his bones and blood vessels. The boy survived the injuries without any long-term damage.

Sometimes, the verbalized chief complaint required interpretation. As an example, an agitated mother stated, "My child was stung by a killer bee." She had heard her four-year-old child cry. He was by himself at a picnic table. The boy said he was stung by something. In the child's past a bee sting caused redness and swelling at the site of envenomation. The mom was concerned that her child might collapse and die as a result of another "aggressive and unprovoked attack."

GO IN PEACE TO HEAL

The thoughts of conscripts and volunteers coincide:
There's joy at mission end for all who adhere
To beliefs that gurney care is o'er bedside
Guard, like non-commissioned under brigadier.
The war is global, so city skirmish or rural foray
Will find you jousting a subarachnoid space,
Halting coronary invasion in electric battle array
Or dueling ventricular amnesia with a pace.
You can prematurely record their defeat in your memoirs.
But before you're branded champion, head this plea!
Cannons are not necessary to chink a patient's armor.
Sensing and responding to hidden agendas are key.
Uncovered fear that you address with calm
Releases a thundering, Heav'n-born balm.

Reprinted from *Academic Emergency Medicine* 7:756, 2000

All doctors listened to the chief complaint. They interpreted the significance of the chief complaint in light of other historical features and correlated this with physical exam findings. Able physicians addressed not only the expressed chief complaint but the unexpressed fear. As a generalization, when you determined a cold was the cause of a child's cough, it was best to indicate in your explanation of findings that you have appropriately excluded pneumonia. This added assurance typically brought visible relief. Your child's headaches weren't caused by a brain tumor. The chest pain was from muscular strain, not a heart attack. Your child's abdominal pain wasn't a result of appendicitis. Or was it?

WE'RE NOT INFALLIBLE

We were told during clinical exposure in medical school that if we practiced emergency medicine for any length of time, we would miss several conditions. These included a heart attack, appendicitis, meningitis, which is an infection of the covering of the brain and intussusception, a mechanical blockage of the bowel. Before the end of my residency I had missed all four of these conditions. I learned valuable lessons from each of the misadventures. Others did as well.

A fellow intern faced a mother who suggested her child's abdominal pain was the result of appendicitis. He indicated the history and physical exam were inconsistent, but the mother insisted this case was identical to her older child's. The older child had been denied the provisional diagnosis of appendicitis and was discharged home from the emergency department. His appendix ruptured. The intern sent her younger child home with instructions to return if the child showed signs and symptoms of deterioration. By the physician's next shift, the child returned with obvious appendicitis.

When I was a senior resident, I was convinced a 7-year-old girl had appendicitis. Dr. Stephen Gelhardt was the surgical intern on-call who responded to my request for a surgical consultation. He evaluated the child and presented to me an argument against the diagnosis of appendicitis. He indicated the child in his opinion could be discharged home. I told him that he needed to contact two individuals. The first was his chief resident, who I was convinced would at least admit the child for continued observation or additional testing. The second person I suggested Stephen contact was a lawyer, because his intentions constituted potential malpractice. "I don't need a lawyer, I am one," he replied as he pulled a business card from his wallet that read *Stephen Gelhardt, M.D., J.D.* Nonetheless, the chief resident overruled Stephen and they found appendicitis at operation.

As much as I wanted to celebrate that success, within the week I had missed establishing the diagnosis of Hirschsprung's disease on an infant that had compatible symptoms. Months after my encounter, she developed toxic megacolon, a known complication of undiagnosed Hirschsprung's disease. Her abdomen suddenly distended, and she developed profuse vomiting and diarrhea. Within hours she went into shock at home. The mother had not recognized how severely her child was impaired. She transported her child to the hospital by the family car. The child was moribund at arrival in the Emergency Department. The old chart was ordered from medical records and arrived coincident with our failure to sustain her life. I opened the record as the child was pronounced dead and was lightning-struck to have recognized the medical history and physical I had previously recorded.

A non-lethal but equally as devastating lightning bolt stuck me when I rendered care to a brother and sister who were victims of a spring tornado. The early morning monstrosity collapsed their home and entrapped family members. I was the sole physician on duty when simultaneously a six-year-old boy and his eight-year-old sister were brought into the E.D. trauma bays by fire fighters. I surveyed both victims, provided immediate direction for the care of both children and went back and forth between the two for several minutes trying to define the extent of their injuries. One gentleman in a fire coat stood silent at the side of the girl, and I announced she was in far greater danger of dying than the boy. Moments later I realized the man I bluntly addressed was the barefooted father in Hanes underwear. He was physically insulated by a loaned fire coat, and I painfully violated his thin veneer.

MEMORABLE ENCOUNTERS WITH ADULTS

We refused no one who sought medical care in the Pediatric E.D. You could count on seeing daily an adult employee who sustained an on-the-job injury or who became unexpectedly ill and was sent to us by their supervisor. We also evaluated complaints in adults visiting hospitalized grandkids, nieces or nephews. With the acute stress on their families, adults overlooked their own health care needs. They forgot to take their own medicines or eat appropriately, and with the freight of seeing a child compromised, the adults decompensated.

Dr. Mike Farrell was in the presence of a visiting grandfather who had a heart attack. Mike initiated a hospital code call and carried on resuscitation during the transport of the gentleman to the E.D. We established an airway, supported his breathing and gave electrical shocks to his heart. We administered Advanced Life Support drugs in the same fashion as for the pediatric patient. That is, we calculated and administered the dose based on the man's body surface area, a reflection of his weight and body habitus. His abnormal heart rhythm stopped. His low blood pressure stabilized. With our treatment, he survived. We transported him by ambulance a half block to University Hospital. The physicians in their E.D. who saw only adult patients laughed when we related our therapeutic approach. They typically provided a syringe full of medication, irrespective of the size of the patient.

We were not trained to care for adults and not comforted by adults collapsing in our presence. In a treatment room of the E.D. while seated on a chair, a grandfather lowered his head when I explained that I had uncovered bacterial meningitis, a potentially life-threatening infection, in his grandchild. I continued my explanation to the four adults in the room until the glasses slipped off the grandad's nose, struck the ground, and his neck remained flexed, his face pointed toward the floor. I palpated his neck, seeking his pulse. I found his carotid heart beat low, but life-sustaining. I stepped out of the treatment room, caught the attention of two nurses and asked them to help me with a code. My voice was controlled, but my own heart raced.

A young lady politely asked for one of our warehoused wheelchairs to transport a volunteer who had "fallen out." This term was used by the public to depict the sudden loss of tone. The most common cause was a faint, so I made no preparations to deal with a calamity. Almost four to five minutes later, the same woman pushed a wide-eyed, anxious silver-haired woman through our entry doors. The elderly but not frail or chronically ill-appearing woman maintained both of her hands at her neck. Her bluish skin color reflected low oxygen in her system. Since we were still in the corridor, I was violating her privacy. However, I sensed urgency.

Facing both women, I asked, "Where have you come from?"

The young woman affirmed my suspicion by reply, "The dining room."

"Can you speak,? I directed to the elder. She shook her head—no.

"Have you choked on something?"

Her wide eyes grew even wider, and she pointed to her throat. I got behind the wheelchair, placed my interlocking hands below her rib cage and thrusted. Nothing happened. I repeated the Heimlich maneuver and out popped a large, partially-chewed piece of meat.

"Thank you," she stated as she negotiated the upright position.

With agility, she stepped over the foot rest of the wheelchair, muttered "I thought I was going to die," and gracefully exited the same door she had been wheeled through moments before.

Dr. Arthur Cornet's mother-in-law, Mary Winton, volunteered twice weekly in the hospital gift shop. Her husband, an esteemed academician, had died years before. Their daughter, Carol, was one of the three women in our medical school class. Carol's interest was in the care of cancer patients, and Art, being of light heart, was trained in pediatrics. The mansion Art and Carol moved into in East Walnut Hills was not quite as run down as the Evanston housing they maintained during their early marriage. They invested their monies and efforts into rehabilitating their master bedroom and bath, then converted the kitchen from a butler's sterile workplace into a warm environment. Then they turned their attention to fixing rooms in a wing of a second floor for Mrs. Winton.

Mrs. Winton parked in the hospital visitor's lot. She negotiated passage from her car to the gated entrance. For some reason, she did not use the sidewalk. When an entering vehicle passed, she avoided contact by as much as four feet. She failed to calculate a safe distance from the descending metal bar. She was struck on the forehead and was knocked unconscious. A passerby saw the accident and summoned a guard.

Mrs. Winton was brought to the Emergency Department. After examining her thoroughly on a cart, I had her sit, stand, then walk before I was convinced she sustained no neck or brain injury from the concussion. I tried twice without success to reach Carol. I called Art.

"This is Singer in the E.D. I was unable to get in touch with your wife. Her mother was knocked unconscious from a descending metal bar parking lot gate and transported here."

"Is she dead?" he asked without any hint of humor.

"No."

"Damn!"

FRIENDS AND CELEBRITIES

Brenda Davis exhibited precocious brilliance in her youth. She skipped a year or two of elementary school and entered Walnut Hills High School at an age from 1 ½ to 2 years younger than others in our class. Not only was she denied by law driving privileges before graduation, she also was biologically deprived of secondary sexual characteristics. Over a decade later when her second-born child developed poor feeding and quit breathing to celebrate his first week of life, he was rushed to the E.D. Brenda's obvious anxiety about an apparent life-threatening event seemed to abate upon seeing me. She was near tears and suffering from a cold. When she first spoke her voice cracked. I replied, "By the sound of your voice, would it be fair to assume that you've finally reached puberty?" She needed the humor.

On an inordinately warm March afternoon, former high school classmate Willa Robertson opened a casement and storm window on the second floor hallway to flood her home with fresh air. Her two-year-old girl awoke from a nap in an adjoining room. Willa saw her for less than a second. Her daughter went from the perched position on the edge to disappearance out the opening. The summoned emergency medical services placed sand bags on both sides of the fallen child's head. They placed wide tape across her forehead and secured her head and neck on a long wooden board. Thin straps were placed to immobilize her body, and additional tape was applied. By the time the squad pulled up to our E.D. her child, Sarah, had almost completely extracted herself. After an exam and repeated assurances to Willa, I permitted Sarah to explore the confines of our trauma room. She took little note of her few superficial abrasions sustained in a 15-foot fall into the shrubbery. Mother needed sedation.

NUTURING THE TRUE E.D. OUTCOME MEASURES

As we relish our communal voice in this thanksgiving eve
Our colleagues are poised in endless invitation to enlarge
A sphere of existence for those courting varied tragedies.
The clever have displayed their relief when those discharged
In no manner return for a differently choreographed diagnosis.
The proficient have sought validation of their response times
And community impact from scrutiny of officiary synopses.
The disciplined, during idleness may draft paradigms
Or polish periods of inaction into sterling algorithms.
The foresighted, who have cultivated brethren physicians
Seldom emerge from a tenuous admit discussion battle-writhed.
Only the foolish ill-plan spiritual relief or key diversions.
Our friends grudgingly accept our cyclical attentions and taciturnity.
At risk are our cherubs; their youth does not endure, but in our memories.

Reprinted with permission from *Academic Emergency Medicine* 2:643,1995

Eileen Sheff and I met in 1964 at the summer camp near Indianapolis. We befriended each other and maintained a relationship for years. I attended her wedding in Mansfield, Ohio and missed her dearly when she moved to California. I became friends with many of her Woodward High School and Ohio State college mates. One of them, Roberta, also settled on the West Coast. In the third year of my residency, Roberta returned with Rita, her first-born, to bond with the Cincinnati grandparents. The infant had been born almost three months prematurely and had an extended hospital stay. She was discharged from the California hospital weighing less than 4 lbs. She was 4 lbs. 10 oz. at the time of her current respiratory illness. Having no Cincinnati source of care, Roberta sought attention for Rita at C.H.M.C. E.D. After we both enjoyed a few minutes of catch-up conversation, I turned my attention to the ex-premie. Roberta undressed her and before redressing Rita in an infant gown, I picked up the naked urchin. Her head and back with small arms fit in my left hand, and in my right hand I supported her bottom and miniature legs. I raised her face to my face, smiled and she squirted a lengthy mustard-consistent pile of excrement in my right hand. I needed soap and water.

Whereas I didn't know the stool was coming, I did get forewarned that the president of the University of Cincinnati was bringing his child for an evaluation of an arm injury sustained on an elementary school playground. Dr. Ed Pratt, who held the highest administrative physician position at C.H.M.C., met the president and his child at the Emergency Department entrance. Dr. Pratt took them through the registration process, then escorted father and child to an examining room. I determined a forearm fracture was likely. Dr. Pratt accompanied them to the Radiology Department where an x-ray film confirmed my suspicion. From the Radiology Department, Dr. Pratt placed a call to Dr. Aaron Pearlman. By the time the three returned from Radiology, Dr. Pearlman was present in the E.D. to cast the child's injury. After discharge instructions were rendered, Dr. Pratt walked them from the premises. Later that afternoon I found a note on my desk. It read, "You obviously have great powers of wisdom and work in a spectacular system that facilitates definitive care and return to productivity all within an hour's time frame. Congratulations on your good work." It was signed, "Ed."

Sports celebrities visited the hospital with frequency. With the exception of Sparky Anderson, who made lengthy day and night visits, other Redlegs passed briefly through our E.D. The Cincinnati Bengals players would exchange a greeting in passing. However, one of the quarterback's kids passed blood in his urine. I was thrilled to explain my findings to a man idolized for his strong throwing arm. A receiver of comparable fame had a child who sporadically suffered asthma attacks. I rendered care on more than one occasion to his boy. One afternoon, I gained his mother's permission to admit him due to a continued need for intravenous medication. I sent her to the admitting office. Shortly thereafter my attentions were disrupted by a knock. In an aggravated tone, I suggested the person enter our treatment room. The tight end took up the entire door frame. I fumbled the intravenous needle.

SHIFT WORK

Part of my altered technical abilities with the young asthmatic patient was a result of performance decrement associated with transitioning from night shifts to day shifts. In pediatric emergency medicine we worked twelve-hour day shifts, ten-hour evening shifts and nine-hour night shifts. Our shifts rotated. It's been well documented that switching shifts in the work place has adverse effects on humans' natural rhythms. All shift workers, especially those who rotate through sporadic periods of night shifts as we did in pediatric emergency medicine, have problems in maintaining consistency in the face of persistent fatigue.

After a string of night shifts, I was out of synch with my environment for days and days. My reaction times, reasoning and mathematical tasks were not to be trusted. My manual dexterity was also suspect during the switch from nights to days. Even if I slept 'til the cows came home following a string of night shifts, I felt sleep deprived and was noticeably inattentive.

In my youth I was not conscious of internal biological rhythms. During my internship and residency, rhythmic phenomena became apparent. Whereas Ruth was an obvious morning person, I was dysfunctional before noon and after midnight. Sex was better after sundown. Morning arousal was present, but efforts to appease Ruth before noon were typically desynchronous. Paralleling sex, my work patterns in the Emergency Department were similar. I was a great noon to midnight doc, but diminished outside this time frame. I was predisposed to problems outside my potent hours.

Before an 11 PM to 8 AM working shift, I took a late afternoon one- to two-hour siesta to "preload" my system. Upon awakening, I generally prayed for God to look after any patients I encountered at 4 AM, because I knew I would not be attentive to their needs. Consistently at 4 AM my mind and/or body forgot the restorative nap I had taken. Inertia hung on my shoulders like a physical weight. I made every effort at 4 AM to anchor myself into any reclining chair. Following such a strategic collapse, I felt refreshed and well adapted to handle whatever the last few hours would bring. If I was deprived of this temporary rest, then determination, courage, curiosity, imagination, collaborative spirit and willingness to care for a suffering fellow human being were imprisoned.

As examples of my 4 AM maladaptation I offer the following three scenarios.

While curled up in a cupboard-sized, irregularly-shaped room in the back of the E.D. that housed reference texts and a telephone, a nurse called me. She had just taken the vital signs on a pre-adolescent female whose mother was concerned about her daughter's state of appearance.

"What's the chief complaint?" I asked.

"The girl's had acute abdominal pain associated with vomiting and diarrhea."

I asked, "Why are you alarmed?"

"Well, her heart rate is only 40 beats/min."

I responded, "Wait five minutes, repeat the heart rate, and if it's again low, do an EKG and call me again."

I hung up the phone but replayed the conversation in my mind before I returned to sleep.

I spoke out loud, "Get your ass out of bed and go see the girl." I did.

Near my witching hour, a preschool-aged child was brought for evaluation of fever. He was clearly ill, and I noted small collections of blood underneath his skin. This is referred to as petechiae, which can accompany serious bacterial infection, including meningitis. After an explanation to his mother, I ordered an appropriate battery of laboratory tests, including a lumbar puncture. In my moment of weakness, I convinced myself the procedure could await the results of his blood studies, urine studies and x-ray of his chest. The hierarchy of values I chose, a half-hour of my recumbency over his potential deterioration, was unconscionable. Fortunately, he suffered no ill effects from my failure to fulfill obligation and perform his lumbar puncture more expeditiously.

In another maladaptation, I was stretched out on two chairs behind a closed door. Kandy knocked to gain my attention. Her voice had a sense of urgency. She stated, "Come quick, we've got a bad one."

I coveted the prestige and authority of my unconscious state. By the time I exited darkness for the glare of the trauma room, three nurses had attended to the child. Kandy had hooked the girl up to monitoring devices and placed a mask on her face, providing extra oxygen. Kandy was establishing an IV.

"Where were you, Jonathan?"

"Jesus, Kandy, I had a boner and couldn't come out of the room!"

Humor hid the true rigidity—my need for sleep.

Night shift work was a major source of stress in other pediatric residents. I was not alone in being disproportionately ineffectual at 4 AM. Others self-selected this time for misbehavior.

Dr. Peter Barnett recorded one encounter that demonstrated his frustration. The Emergency Department medical record was signed by one of the nurses in attendance who wrote, "I have witnessed the above and concur with the findings."

Barnett's medical record stated, "17-year-old white female with 1 ½ week history of sore throat, swollen glands without fever. No other problems. No limitation activity. Patient resting comfortably without fast breathing and absolutely in no distress. Asked if her private doctor notified. Mom said she wouldn't do that at this time in the morning. I asked why she would bother us but not him, whether she knew this was an emergency department for emergency and acute care. I asked her whether she had insurance or was paying for this. She said this was a *life and death situation* and that I was paid to care for her daughter. I told her I thought this was an unwise use of an emergency facility and that I would be glad to see her daughter anyway. I left the room, asking the patient to gown for the exam. When the nurse entered the room, the mother began yelling and screaming, said she hoped I would die of a heart attack and left before my evaluation (despite the life and death situation)."

As demonstrated above, the late-night use of the pediatric emergency department for nonacute or nonurgent conditions could generate problems for some residents in training. Rather than spending time addressing medical issues, too many residents on night shifts asked why the parent decided to bring the child to the E.D. at the particular time of presentation and not earlier or later. I recognized during my internship that there were many medical or non-medical reasons that drove parents to the emergency department at odd hours. I felt it was not necessary to learn the motivation for parents who brought children for care beyond their usual bedtime. From my point of view, it did not matter whether their concerns for the visit were valid from my standpoint. If their visit occurred at a time when we had reduced staffing by physicians, nurses, clerks and aides, reduced capacity for ancillary care (respiratory therapy, radiology or laboratory), we had to do our best. It was the public's perception that we were there for any medical and surgical emergencies, significant trauma, lessor injuries or minor medical problems. The public expected us to diagnose their children in a timely fashion and render treatment, irrespective of the time of day.

When a mother brought her 13-year-old son to the department at 3

AM for a painful swelling under his left breast, noted for a six-month time frame, I was not disturbed. The young man had a history and physical to suggest features of a benign variant of normal breast development. My assumption was that the mother thought the child may have had a serious underlying condition, such as breast cancer. I did not chastise her for abusing the service for the sake of convenience. I did not inventory her cultural belief systems, her relationship with a private practitioner or determine the family's illness experience with breast disease. I politely addressed their concern. They indicated their appreciation. Had they come one hour later they would have seen my maladaptive biophysiologic state in all its glory.

PRIVATE PRACTICE

Medicine beyond midnight was practiced more over the telephone than in face to face encounters by pediatricians in private practice. Private practitioners of pediatrics had graduated from pediatric internship and residency programs and established an office in a community of their choice. Their office may have been a traditional medical building or some other facility converted to a waiting room and examining rooms. Private practitioners provided medical care from within the walls of their office, typically from morning through early evening. When the door closed, they accepted inquiries by concerned parents until the doors opened again the next morning. How often a private practitioner fielded night questions was generally a function of the size of their partnerships. If four pediatricians worked together from an office and they equally shared night calls, the potential for medical decisions beyond midnight came every four nights. A three-person group rotated every third, and a two-person group rotated call every other night. The person in solo practice committed to a continuous availability status unless multiple solo practitioners banded together to cross cover additional practices on a rotational basis.

Parental inquiries were directed to the on-call physician by cities' medical societies or other answering services. The physician would ask a battery of questions in an effort to determine if the child needed to be evaluated now or whether the hands-on exam could be delayed until the morning office hours. If a decision was made that an immediate assessment should be carried out, the practitioner would direct the parent and child to meet them at the locked office door, or to meet them at a close at hand community E.D. If the pediatrician wanted to extract themselves from a face to face encounter, they could direct the patient to a community E.D. or to the Children's Hospital Emergency Department. The community E.D.s were staffed by individuals who had recently completed emergency medicine training. The Children's Hospital emergency department was staffed by pediatric interns and residents in training. The pediatrician had to either trust an emergency medicine physician who may not have had significant exposures to sick kids during residency training or a potentially naive pediatric intern or resident who had no immediate supervision.

By my third year of pediatric residency, I had been repeatedly on the receiving end of children sent to the E.D. late night for assessment. I had not experienced decision-making from the perspective of a private practitioner. Midway through the year, private physicians that I admired consented to my brief apprenticeship. I arranged to spend a working week in four different pediatric offices.

Dr. Roger Giessel established an office among one of Cincinnati's eastern strip mall storefronts. He was a solo practitioner who was best known for his yearly impersonation of Santa Claus, who seasonally visited in full attire the infirm at the hospital. He dispensed gifts, but more importantly gave of himself. He was equally giving in his preceptorship for a week. I found his devotion to medicine admirable, but his demanding lifestyle destructive.

Dr. Tom Forristal, youthful in appearance, had long sustained execessive work stresses of prolonged solo practice. He was jubilant during my week, celebrating the recent arrival of his first partner into his rural practice. Tom enthusiastically treated each patient sequestered in a treatment room. He engaged the mother and child equally and addressed appropriate healthcare needs for well child visits. He left open periods in between well child encounters and saw sick visitors. For his routine on sick patients Tom examined the children, determined the nature of the problem and wrote nothing in the chart. A nurse entered, Tom told her the diagnosis, then he left the room. The nurse wrote in the patient's chart, created a prescription, explained the anticipated course of the illness and helped secure a follow-up appointment. All the while, Tom was in the next treatment room taking the history and performing the physical examination. The nurse joined him, and the process repeated itself. If the nurse was delayed, Tom went to his desk and tackled a receptionist-generated running log of needed telephone calls. Over lunch, Tom ate a brown bag lunch and made further telephone calls. One would think this indigestible pace was impossible to emulate.

Dr. Joe Cionni's operational events bore uncanny resemblance to Tom Forristal's. Joe had a partner and was seeking a third person in order to serve a rapidly-growing practice in the western extremes of Cincinnati. Joe and his partner held court for their pediatric care in a house converted for medical use. Their anticipated newly-constructed office did alleviate a lot of their physical congestion. However, the pace of encounters remained frantic. Joe felt they needed to squeeze in visits for anyone who called with a concern. He was facile at directing the concentrated effort at the expressed chief complaint. With the brevity of each encounter, he discouraged discussion of tangential medical issues, except the status of family relationships.

Izzy Kadetz, a restauranteur in downtown Cincinnati, manned the cash register of his delicatessen. His establishment maintained no billing slips. He queried the customer regarding their meal as they departed. He asked what they ate for lunch and arbitrarily determined a price for the meal, based on whether or not he liked you, how he felt about your palate or how he valued your potential for a repeat visit. Dr. Joe Cionni was like Izzy Kadetz, favoring the patron who had chosen a hot corned beef on rye and punishing the soul who mistakenly chose turkey on white bread. Upon departing the room, Joe fixed a dollar amount on the charge for the office visit. For the same service with an identical consumption of time, the price fluctuated. The amount Joe charged seemed to be low for large families, lower for children who had a chronic disease state, and lowest if Joe felt you loved your kids. Puzzled by my inquisitive look, Joe confided the charge for one dad was near nothing because "he teaches in the parochial school system and is devoted to his six kids."

Drs. Devoe, DeGarmo, Lichtenberg and Bobbitt took the high end food court approach to their practice. The four were accessed through the same entry door within a medical complex in north central Cincinnati. Yet each ran a separate practice, with their own patients, their own examining rooms, nursing and clerical staff. Senior partner Dr. Devoe set the example for a group that, in my mind, had mastered a unique style. He was thorough in his medical care. He sustained the body language that suggested no need to retreat. The patient before him appeared to be his sole priority. Parents and children appreciated his conversational tone. He anticipated questions, encouraged dialogue and generated advice. He charted his own information, wrote his own prescriptions, and gave his own immunizations and injections. He rarely troubled his nurse, who spent the majority of her day on the telephone. Dr. Devoe only touched the implement every fourth evening in response to night inquiries.

NO SMALL BUSINESS

Dr. Devoe valued his time at no greater or lesser an hourly rate compared to the other practitioners. Because he took more time per patient, he charged more per encounter. In contrast to Dr. Cionni, Dr. Devoe's cost was fixed, irrespective of family dynamics. Dr. Devoe's fees were established by his business office. The business office determined the fixed cost of the operation (gas, electricity, rental of space, etc.), and established fees for service that guaranteed a profit for the corporation if greater than 90% of the families paid their bills within three billing cycles.

In my month of preceptorship, I acquired some medical insights, but the most meaningful information these learned physicians transmitted was financial. In my naivete I had entered their private practice domain seeking to learn how they reduced diagnostic uncertainty when faced with a sick child in their office setting. Instead, they emphasized how to profit as a business. They taught me an immunization strategy for a child lacking certain shots rested in part on the probability of being reimbursed for those immunizations. Payment histories were prominently affixed to medical records. Discretionary requests for co-payment for services currently rendered were made based on prior payment histories. As if they felt compelled, the physicians taught me how to reuse disposable equipment, waste fewer paper towels, build my own examining table and communicate more efficiently with fewer telephone outlets.

In order to remain efficient, each practice, irrespective of physician size, averaged three to four equivalent, full-time employees per physician. With smooth-running business systems and ample personnel in place, the salary costs, which averaged 23% of gross receipts, were an acceptable evil. The doctors and their office managers stressed the benefit of paying straight salary to multiple part-time employees to perform the workload of one person. Apparently, if you reduced the duty hours below a critical figure, you avoided the high cost of Workmen's Compensation, retirement contributions and other traditional fringes. Money managers accepted volatility of multiple personalities partially employed, over a single person's mastery of skill, for a savings from 1.3 to 2.9% of gross receipts.

From my limited observations of several family-run businesses, work satisfaction and productivity were maximal when smaller numbers of long-term employees knowledgeable of everyone's tasks provided service. The proliferative fill-in employee concept was counterintuitive. But then I knew my inherent business sense was also a product of my own family's unrefined inefficiencies. Pop had projected a price for his services based on gut feel. He rounded off the state's requirements of taxation to a close approximation. He was not concerned with details and sometimes failed to follow Mom's stringent criteria of charging enough to cover our own costs. Pop continued to produce work for people with an aggregate debt as long as he felt they were not taking advantage of his *laissez faire* business attitude.

I may have had the attitude and medical skills for private practice, but by month's end I knew the lack of business sense would hamper my transition to their activities. The success of my career could not be based on my acquisition of a pre-subscribed financial curriculum. I demanded an occupation preferentially dominated by need for a service and free of dictated charges under my control. The concept of providing clinical care in C.H.M.C.'s E.D. while overseeing the unsupervised care provided by residents in return for salary was implanted on my brain.

ASPIRING TO A CAREER

BIRTHING

A pediatric internship and residency readied a physician to render care for patients from birth through early adulthood. Theoretically, the adequately trained pediatrician was capable of dealing with any problem during this time frame. However, some medical events were so complex or occurred so infrequently in the course of a general practice of pediatrics that parent and pediatricians alike turned to subspecialists for help.

Pediatric subspecialists have engaged in training beyond the residency, concentrating their studies of a particular body system such as the heart (cardiologist), bowel (gastroenterologist), etc. In order to facilitate their focused, in-depth understanding, medical centers offered fellowships in these subspecialty areas. The available fellowships offered structured curriculums with educational experiences that lasted two to three years. The fellowships offered lectures, discussion groups, demonstrations, laboratory experiences, specific readings and bedside teaching. These critical lessons and administrative issues were under the direct supervision of an experienced physician, who was held in esteem by their colleagues for their unique perspective in the domain covered by the fellowship.

In 1975, at the time I completed my pediatric residency, no medical centers offered a fellowship in pediatric emergency medicine. For me, there were no available apprenticeships. I therefore sought the advice and direction of both Drs. Pratt and Schubert. These senior physicians at C.H.M.C. accepted my proposal for career development. We devised a year-long template of self-study. I learned how to focus a majority of my attentions within the emergency setting. I refined my own priorities of care based on rapid recognition and management of life- and limb-threatening conditions. I also defined how I would function within C.H.M.C.'s organizational structure. C.H.M.C. financially sponsored this year of extended training under the umbrella they referred to as an Ambulatory Fellowship. A few colleagues with similar interests in other parts of the country sought attainment of similar knowledge. The first program in the U.S. that provided identity for pediatric emergency medicine as an area of subspecialty began in 1980. The first fellows of pediatric emergency medicine (P.E.M.) like me joined the full-time faculty at academic centers.

In 1976, I joined the full-time academic faculty at C.H.M.C. The University of Cincinnati provided me the title of Assistant Professor of Pediatrics and Emergency Medicine. Like all other full-time faculty members, I was held to three specific expectations. The first foundation in professional life was service to the hospital, the medical school and the university. The second commitment was student-centered learning. The third leg of the professional stool was scholarship.

BEDSIDE TEACHING ROLE

All the while my self-tutorial prioritization skills evolved, I supervised students and residents who rotated for one month intervals through the E.D. I worked to improve their clinical proficiency by working side by side with them. Rather than attempting to be a reservoir of random knowledge, I tried to make the practice of medicine understandable and meaningful. I tried to personalize any teaching and tie information to patient care experiences. I made attempts to maximize teaching opportunities by bringing concurrently-working physicians to the bedside of any child whose example provided instruction. I sought the level of comfort of the parent and the child with the concept of sharing their history or their physical examination findings. If they consented, I introduced them to students and residents in training. I appreciated patients and parents who relished the concept of advancing knowledge of well-intended students. In exchange for facilitating these real-life examples of both common and uncommon illness, I showered the parent-child unit with thanks.

Not long after our impromptu class, the families probably forgot the lesson. However, I am convinced the learners, engaged in the human-to-human experience, long remembered the value of the tutorial. As an example, I suspect Howard, a third-year medical student, remembers multiple years after the encounter the circumstance where I introduced him to a young man whose heart was transposed before birth to the right side of his chest by a quirk of nature. I had sought permission to share the child's complaint of fever, cough and congestion. I instructed the family not to divulge the birth defect and pulled Howard into the room. Howard was told to take the history, perform the physical examination before me and come to a diagnosis. In attentive silence, I stood in the corner while Howard elicited a rich and accurate patient history directed at excluding various respiratory ailments. I faced Howard, maintained intermittent eye contact and nodded in approval as Howard struggled by his exam to diagnose a major lung problem. At the end, Howard was perplexed. The family and I had a sparkle in the eye and a light step divulging the diagnosis of a cold in a child with a normal heart located in the right rather than left chest.

For awake, alert children beyond a year or so of life, I tried to balance their growing need for privacy. I measured their potential embarrassment of exposure versus the potential teaching impact. As an example, a 5-year-old boy had pain in his groin as a result of a twisted structure riding high on the top of his right testicle. The torsion of his testicular appendage created a blue coloration that was visible through the wall of his scrotal sac. The boy's scrotum had a classic "blue dot" appearance. This blue dot sign is described in textbooks but rarely seen in practice. The boy had been advised by his parents to never display his genitals before anyone outside of his family. The boy was reluctant to share his genitals before me, a single doctor. His parents understood from my enthusiasm there was opportunity for illuminating others present in the department. With their blessing and after a full explanation, we repressed the content of the young man's previous genital lessons, and he accommodated the oogling eyes of no less than four other doctors.

At our maximal patient volume, no more than six doctors were scheduled to be present in the department. In order to share similar clinical implements of instruction with large numbers of students and residents not present, I captured other encounters with a still or video camera.

I was forewarned by a paramedic squad over telemetry that they were en route with a 4-year-old young man with a butter knife stuck in the roof of his mouth. I met the squad at the ambulance entrance with camera in hand. "Before we do anything, I *have* take a picture," I explained with a sense of pleading.

The father said, "Only if you take a second one for me."

I did, and his son was ultimately shared with the entire medical community as I wrote the child's case history as part of a published manuscript on emergency management of mouth injuries in children. His child had been running from his older brother who was in pursuit of an apple. The little brother was using a knife to spread peanut butter on the apple. He did not wish to share. He ran with the knife in his mouth, tripped and impaled the knife deeply into the back of his throat. After assuring patency of the child's airway, I acquired an x-ray that confirmed the blade's penetration to China. Both the photo of the child and the x-ray live forever as teaching tools.

For placement in our major trauma room, I purchased a video camera. At the beginning of my shift, I sat the tripod on a corner desk with the camera face pointed at the trauma bay bed. When a severely ill or injured child was placed in the trauma bay, I let the camera roll. At a later date, I viewed our treatment. I made an assessment determining whether we provided efficient, quality and compassionate care. In a small group setting, I showed edited tapes that ultimately promoted protocol development and quality assurance mechanisms.

The video camera was rolling when a neurosurgical resident responded to our need for consultation. A critically ill child was brought by life squad when parents found the child seizing. The father, enraged by persistent crying, had violently shaken the child into submission. We were not aware of the "shaken baby syndrome." The child had physical findings to suggest massive swelling of the brain. We were under the hypothesis that the child seized because of spontaneous bleeding into the area adjacent to the brain substance. This condition, called subdural hematoma, would shortly be diagnosable by an imaging device called Computerized Tomography (C.T.), which was under development. Before the equipment was available, we diagnosed subdural hematoma through demonstration of blood in the subdural spaces. The neurosurgeon, at our request, prepared the skin over the child's soft spot (fontanel) and inserted needles sequentially into the right and left subdural spaces. Before he placed the needles through the skin, he looked up at my camera, made an off-color remark, stuck his tongue out at me and danced a jig. Several hours later the child died while in our I.C.U. The father was ultimately tried for child abuse. I was concerned the tape would be played before a jury and cast an inappropriate light on our medical care. I videotaped more selectively.

On occasion, I found myself ill-equipped to memorialize an image. I called upon others with greater expertise. I was out of film in my camera on a day when a youngster presented with a black coating on her tongue. The number of conditions creating a black tongue are limited. In her case, it was due to ingestion of Pepto-Bismol. The bismuth salicylate created the change on her tongue. I asked the hospital's medical photographer to take a photo. She arrived, took several pictures and departed before I could thank her. Four to five hours later, she was leaving the hospital. I passed her in the hallway. She was among three women, two respiratory therapists and a nurse. I tapped her on the shoulder and continued to walk. I raised my hand, caught her eye, and blinked to convey my thanks. I kept walking and then heard in reply, "Great tongue, Dr. Singer."

I stopped and said, "I won't touch that line with a 10-foot pole."

A tongue, like every body part, has a role to play in health. During sickness, changes that may occur could be captured on photo or film and shared at a later date. Occasionally, some findings had to be immediately brought before the widest possible audience. When this occurred, I contacted every available resident in the hospital. A child with an acutely dysfunctional tongue created urgency for such a teaching moment.

A less-than-2-year-old male found his brother's attention deficit hyperactivity disorder medication. Like many preschoolers, he negotiated the top off a child-proof bottle. He ingested between six to eight tablets of Cylert. Mother discovered the ingestion several hours later and brought the boy to the Emergency Department. The toddler was awake and alert with minimal alteration in his vital signs. He looked oddly at his trunk and extremities. He incessantly picked at his skin as if he were displacing a colony of ants that mounted him for pleasure. His tongue slightly protruded and took on a life of its own. The apparatus was seemingly demonized and moved in uncontrollable fits. Resources of information available to me suggested that brief hallucination and uncontrolled body movements had been reported following large-dose ingestion of Cylert. We kept our eye on him in the department and watched all symptoms resolve. Before he went home, I shared his altered state with close to 50 physicians. All watched in fascination, and they hopefully retained the educational aspect of the sideshow.

The ultimate purpose of faculty-directed bedside supervision was to bring the physicians-in-training to a point of functioning independently. No matter how accomplished I or any of the faculty supervisors were in our roles, patients, more than teachers, extended the students' repertoire of knowledge. In adult emergency medicine training, I had seen too many of their teachers unwittingly drawn to severely ill patients. From my perspective, every patient, no matter how ill, had the potential for a teaching soliloquy.

GRADUATED MEASURE OF BLISS

Within hours of celebration we'll receive a half look,
Over the shoulder motion as your story's suspended.
Chronicled monthly reports become dormant books
Of classics, earmarked for impact that's unended.
Measuring the fare forward, you seek successor's victory;
Pioneers have been fulfilled by opportunity to resolve
A fusion of past years' disease or mindless reverie.

It's a pulse to guard against forces of unaltered law!
Yes, there's artistry attending a monitored isle
Withholding emotion as momentum shifts downward.
Yet thc brush strokes of resurrection and greatest rewards
Attend the clasp of a hand in fast track, delivered with style.

Reprinted from *Academic Emergency Medicine* 5:857, 1998

INSUFFICIENT SPACE

Patients were needed. The questioned remained—how many? Too few provided little opportunity for learning emergency pediatric care. However, our problem was too many patients for the space provided. Plans for rehabilitating C.H.M.C.s existing E.D. were initiated in the late 1960s, at a time when there were 6,000-7,200 yearly visits. The year during remodeling brought 9,000 patients, and 14,000 sought care within a year of construction. Within another year, I joined the faculty, and the future projected maximal volume of 22,000 patient encounters was exceeded. Over subsequent years, the volume grew at a pace that approximated 9,000 additional visits per year. By 1980, 72,000 visits made C.H.M.C. the second busiest pediatric E.D. in the nation.

The non-patient care facilities in the front of the E.D. were insufficient, and the layout of the area violated the senses. There was a single, common entrance door for patients brought by family car or by ambulance. At peak hours, the front door bottleneck projected a less-than-pleasant, caring image. Those who entered the overcrowded milieu were met by registration clerks. They were responsible for extracting demographic information (including insurance information) and the chief complaint. These invasions of privacy were carried out over a counter top within earshot of anyone navigating a public passageway. Registration clerks passed the completed E.D. chart to an in basket for perusal by a nurse. Patients and their guardians were advised to sit in the E.D. waiting area adjacent to Registration. Children with infectious diseases were inadequately separated from those with injuries. All waited in a huddled environment until a care area opened up in the back of the department.

Sporadically, a nurse picked up a chart from the in basket, faced the general direction of the assemblage, and in resounding town crier fashion, called out the patient's name. The patient was escorted through an unsecured door, and the parent-child unit was invited to sit on molded plastic chairs lining the hallway. While exposed to all traffic, the same nurse took a history as well as measured the breathing rate, heart rate and weight. The nurse then took either an oral or rectal temperature, depending upon the child's age.

The patient-parent unit was invited to sit on another set of chairs somewhere in the hallway or in an enclosed patient care room. The site of placement for patient care depended upon both the nature of the problem, the availability of room space, and the likelihood of prompt or delayed arrival of the treating physician.

The majority of patients were placed in a 6-foot by 8-foot standard room that housed a gurney, frequently used wall-mounted equipment, a sink and a set of cabinetry containing less frequently used supplies. Six nearly identical standard rooms branched in succession from a T-shaped hallway. Patients with isolated injuries or breathing problems unlikely to require additional oxygen were evaluated in the unprotected environment of central hallway chairs.

There was a tendency to accumulate patients with a common theme in an intersecting back hallway. Depending upon the season and the time of day, the recruitment for the back hallway varied. Year around, the most common type of back hallway patient had sustained a laceration or had a documented fracture. Typically, those with diagnosed broken bones were corralled outside the 14-foot by 16-foot orthopedic room, and those with lacerations were sequestered outside the 16-foot by 16-foot suture room. However, the herds were interrupted by patients who remained in the recesses of the back hallway until the in-hospital nursing staff was able to accept them for admission, and any patient who we provided prolonged emergency care.

Few events induced a stampede, but anyone with a life-threatening illness or injury was brought through this back hallway crowd into the trauma room. The 15-foot by 20-foot potential area bounded by walls was more confined by cabinetry stocked with resuscitation drugs and surgical supplies. The room amply served any patient needing comprehensive care rendered by one or two physicians and up to three nurses. Rarely was any patient an ultimate beneficiary of more than five caretakers. However, the floor space would not permit a sustained presence by more than five providers if they were needed.

WORKING WITH THE CONTROLLERS

Dr. Mark McGovern completed his residency at C.H.M.C. several years before me. He acquired additional knowledge and experience in the Northwest, and then returned to be Director of Ambulatory Care. Mark was responsible for the Ambulatory Clinics and the Emergency Department. Mark named me Director of the E.D., but as my supervisor, he never defined my job description in writing. Without question, we were both responsible for supervising patient care and teaching. Neither of us knew the extent of our administrative roles, and each attempt to rectify a perceived problem was a trip through unnavigated waters.

Alaine Barsan, R.N., was the living caricature of a Norman Rockwell painting. She carried herself with pride about the hospital in starched dress, nursing cap, stockings and shoes. This apparition in white-on-white was seen day and night. She lived on the hospital premises and devoted her life to nursing care at the hospital. Her knowledge of pediatric nursing was as vast as the Kansas wheat fields of her youth. She was held in high esteem by nursing subordinates who respected her role as Nursing Director. She inspired all with machine-like stamina, unnatural for her advancing age. Unfortunately, she was as forward-thinking as the farmer unwilling to forego the mule for a diesel engine. Entrenched in opinion, she was psychologically akin to the animal in question. Anyone, nurse or physician alike, who wished to advance patient care through nursing innovation had to first appease Miss Barsan.

Being committed to change, being naive, and possessing a zest for battle, I locked horns in a friendly fashion with Miss Barsan. With luck and an unusual strength of purpose, I succeeded on several fronts with Alaine. Ideas and proposals were converted to realities. Miss Barsan permitted the E.D. nurses to perform blood draws, start IV lines and administer breathing treatments. These liberties were not extended to equally-trained or procedurely-competent nurses elsewhere in the hospital. E.D. nurse shifts were amended from the traditional 7 AM-3 PM, 3 PM-11 PM, 11 PM-7 AM maintained elsewhere in the hospital. The nurses staggered their arrival times, maximizing their presence as our patient volume swelled. E.D. nurses underwent a structured training for patient triage. The trained triage nurses replaced the receptionist as the first to greet the parent-patient unit at the emergency entrance. We cleared out two cupboards, which permitted the triage nurse to acquire a history and take vital signs in seclusion. Miss Barsan approved the nurse's selection of a smock and pants to replace a dress uniform.

Despite repeated courteous probing and intellectually stimulating arguments, Miss Barsan blocked several paths of my laudable pursuits. She would not dilute the educational background of the E.D. staff. Newly-hired nurses had to be Registered Nurses. I perceived that more bodies were needed for lower-level decision-making tasks such as fluid sample transportation, patient transportation to x-ray and hospital floors, and holders for medical procedures. In my estimate, a higher salary cost was being incurred for labors typically performed by a Licensed Practical Nurse or a Nurse's Aide. Miss Barsan would also not support the specific training and permanent employment of physician assistants (P.A.), who could have facilitated more rapid care of orthopedic patients with fractures and patients with lacerations. Other hospitals and medical literature had proven the cost-effective wisdom of P.A. utilization in the environment of the emergency department. Miss Barsan accepted in-hospital floor nurse appeals over Emergency Department nurses regarding admissions. She granted the floor nurses the authority to block transportation of an admitted patient from the E.D. to the floor. In principle, Miss Barsan did not want a parent to be escorted *nea*r to an area of definitive care but not reach the ultimate room space. Rather than waiting in a holding pattern on the floor, she preferred the ineffectual and overflowing runway of our Emergency Department back hallway.

Miss Barsan also misconstrued the fracturing impact of firing Linda, an E.D. nurse with years of experience, who had brought relief, comfort and support to thousands of patients. Linda, a perennially smiling imp, profited from living in a log cabin. She gained insights from open relationships with people from all walks of life. She easily merged the pleasures in her personal life with professional joys. She more than adequately fulfilled all nursing obligations and had chronically merited accolades on her formal job assessments. Her persistent failure to wear a brassiere initially gained Miss Barsan's informal comment. Written notification, repeat demand, threat and ultimately dismissal followed. For Miss Barsan, compassion for the ailing was secondary to the guided, uplifting from underwear.

Lyle Mills, C.H.M.C.'s Hospital Administrator responsible for the Ambulatory Department and E.D., was also clothes conscious. Although he was informal within the confines of his office, for forays outside he buffed his cordovan wing tips and donned his suit jacket. Lyle expanded evening clerical coverage in the hospital's Admitting Office. He secured desk space and funding for a clerk in the back of the E.D. The clerk manned phone lines, improving our internal and external communications. Lyle initiated and chaired formal monthly meetings between the E.D. head nurse, a pediatric surgeon, a clerical representative, myself, and Miriam Katz, the hospital's Patient Advocate. We addressed problems as a matter of routine. Unfortunately, Lyle was too conscious of superficial appearance. He generally chose a simple solution, even if the result was ineffectual, if it looked good, particularly in the eyes of his supervisors.

Miriam Katz spent over 30 years seeking feedback from the public who utilized the hospital's services. As wife of a rabbi, she ably performed crisis intervention and emotional support when hospital clergy were not present. Miriam saw her main role as the source for maintenance of patients' rights. She was an accessible source of referral and information, long working out of an alcove off the Emergency Department entry.

With Lyle's help, we relocated Miriam, divided her prized floor space with kiosks, and accomplished patient registration in private. As if in retribution, in the privacy of my office, Miriam often came with chart in hand to discuss an emergency case that had come to her attention. The problems the consuming public found repeatedly objectionable were overbilling, prolonged wait for appropriate emergency care, expeditious but inappropriate care and inordinate delays until reaching the ultimate bed space for patients admitted to the hospital floor.

OVERBILLING

Nationwide in the 1970's, one in ten to fifteen outpatient hospital bills contained inappropriate requests for reimbursement. From various estimates, C.H.M.C. had an equivalent rate of inaccuracies. However, from the frequency of errors Miriam brought to my office, I projected a more pervasive problem. For example, a physician ordered a pregnancy test on an adolescent female who presented to the E.D. with acute abdominal pain. The $12.00 urine pregnancy test was performed, but the patient was charged $120 for a urine pregnentriol level, which was a study requiring shipment of frozen urine to an Endocrinology Lab in southern California. When I explored the details, I learned the overcharge by a factor of 10 was the result of an inputting clerical error within the computer-based charging system.

By the time I investigated too many to count billing complaints, I marveled at our institution's capacity to err. Ultimately, I took a step-by-step analysis of our charges. After inquiries at every administrative office that potentially provided ancillary billable services to an emergency patient, discussions with a billing programmer, tutorials by the billing inputer and the accounts receivable office, it was apparent to me that the desire for the hospital to dispense a bill within 72 hours of service caused a high error rate. With data in hand from a lengthy audit, I created a position paper depicting the solutions and sought a meeting with Morton Gullickson, the Hospital Administrator who dealt with collections. Morton, in everyone's estimate, was a handsome, bland yes-man in formal attire who sought equanimity over innovation. He listened intently to my conversation and then advised me that any solution that lead to a single day's delay return of money to the hospital was fiscally unsound. My concept of delaying the billing for 36 additional hours to ensure accuracy by a two-step cross check was untenable. Morton denied every contested error in billing ultimately delayed reimbursement for a minimum of three to six months. Further, he denied the 22% error rate during my report was unrepresentative of reality. He was not swayed by arguments. He led me out of his office emotionally patting me on the head and suggested I "stick with doctoring," as he closed the door to reason.

PROLONGED WAITS

A pediatric surgeon with international renown headed the pediatric surgical service. A cadre of finely-skilled pediatric surgeons were promptly responsive to most of our surgical needs in the Emergency Department. When called by us for a child who got entangled with rotating bladed farm equipment or a child with a severe burn, they or their surgical residents arrived in moments. The exception for responsiveness was for patients with lacerations.

Those patients with scalp lacerations or split chins were lowest in the surgeon's priorities. Patients needing laceration repair were to be treated by the staff surgeon, surgical fellow, or by surgical resident. A child who presented early in the morning for a laceration repair might have waited until noon if the surgeons were tied up with surgical cases in the Operating Room. A child unfortunate enough to arrive about noon was likely to be housed in the E.D. lobby or back hallway until 4:00 p.m. At that time, a surgical resident who was off duty from his other responsibilities "moonlighted" until midnight. The moonlighting resident was paid a flat fee of $100.00 to be present for eight hours and $10.00 per case for laceration repair.

The head of the Pediatric Orthopedic Department possessed a well-deserved reputation for excellence. He was internationally known for rehabilitation of children with complex disease states. He had trained under another expert who taught him that almost all fracture care could wait. Unless a patient with a fracture had a bone sticking through the skin, or there was loss of blood supply to the area beyond the fracture, the fracture treatment could wait. In the E.D., we temporarily splinted injuries and provided pain control until the orthopedist arrived to provide definitive care.

The hospital's Chief Administrator was aware of our dilemma with the surgeons and the orthopedists. He asked me to document circumstances where there were lengthy delays. I sent a letter a week later providing a narrative of the "latest orthopedic atrocity." Rather than raising a general philosophical question with the orthopedist, the Chief Administrator shared my actual letter. I had not expected the ambush by the Chief Administrator. The orthopedist was upset by my characterizations of his department's care. After he demanded my explanation of written comments, we got along quite well, but patients with pain and deformity from fractures still lingered too long in our E.D. awaiting definitive care.

INAPPROPRIATE CARE

Vivian, a premedical undergraduate student from the University of Cincinnati volunteering on weekends in our suture room, shyly approached me the day after she witnessed a transgression. By her account, the moonlighting surgical resident on a hot Sunday summer evening was visibly stressed by unremitting laceration repairs. A youngster, who was not pleased with the pain incurred during infiltration of his laceration with the numbing medication, broke free from Vivian's restraint. The child bit the surgical resident. Vivian suggested the child's behavior was understandable, but when the surgical resident bit the child back, Vivian thought the adult had breached a standard of care.

I thanked Vivian for bringing the event to my attention. The experience had obviously disturbed her, and she contemplated keeping the story to herself. It was not easy for her to see both sides of the issue. The surgical chairman and I concurred the reflexive action of the exhausted and harried surgical resident was not an acceptable excuse for child abuse, but at least there was some excuse. The following events had none.

A six-year-old child tripped on the entrance stairs to elementary school. He fell on an outstretched elbow. Mother retrieved the previously-healthy child and brought him to the E.D. After registration, the child had vital signs taken and was escorted to a back hallway chair. He was examined in a chair, and a doctor ordered the patient to be taken to the basement Radiology suite for an x-ray of his elbow. While still sitting, the mother and child were approached by a nurse who failed to check the child's wristband. The nurse asked if this was Richard, and both the mother and child communicated something that led the nurse to believe she had identified the correct patient with asthma. The nurse ungraciously lifted the child's broken arm he had been protecting, and gave the child a shot of adrenalin for an asthma attack.

A question was raised that a ten-year-old with a vaginal discharge was chronically sexually assaulted. The child was placed in the standard examining room made special by a table containing stirrups. The physician was able with explanation, to look within the child's vagina by using equipment that was manufactured for veterinary use. The veterinary doctors used very long but skinny tubes to perform ear exams on horses and cattle. You could painlessly insert the veterinary plastic devices into a child's vagina, send light down the instrument and use swabs to collect specimens from anatomy in your full view. The child in question seemed to have a malodorous discharge resulting from retained toilet paper. Cultures for various venereal diseases were sent to the lab for anticipated results within 48 hours. The child and her escort were sent home, and one nurse changed the bed sheet. The veterinary instruments were still resting on the counter adjacent to the sink when another prepubescent child was brought into the room by another nurse. The resident physician entered shortly thereafter and asked multiple questions directed at determining the possible cause of the child's vaginal bleeding. A nurse assisted the child into a stirrupped position. The physician used the same veterinary equipment that had not been sterilized from the previous encounter.

DELAYED ADMISSIONS

Over the three years of my residency training, more patients destined for admission were sent by their physicians through the Emergency Department. The clerical, nursing and physician staff expedited as best they could the diagnostic studies and therapeutic interventions for patients who had been seen by their doctors and deemed ill enough for admission. The staff was also on the lookout for potential admissions among those who utilized the E.D. as their primary source of care. In both circumstances, patients immediately identified by triage at high risk for deterioration were often recipients of care in the patient care area even before registrars generated a chart. But even with our heightened concerns for admittable patients we caused delays.

When admission procedures were completed, unnecessary delays in the eyes of the parent occurred. All admitted patients were delayed by the duplicate re-registration process in the Admitting Office. The E.D. computers, for reasons I never understood, could not interface with Admitting's computers. Admitted patients who needed x-rays were sent to the basement, one floor and several hallways away. These patients were interdigitated between other outpatients and inpatients sent by their doctors for imaging procedures. This also created delay. We were a system of bottle necks.

I interviewed 100 parents by visitation to the floor the day following admission of their children. At my request, they completed a survey. The results showed that parents recognized our E.D. nurse and physician attention as focused, prompt and complete. The parents felt definitive care was started in the E.D. They were disturbed by our flow and inefficiencies, but they did not perceive the delay reaching the hospital floor resulted in delay in definitive care for their child.

For one month, I tracked the entire time course for over 600 patients admitted through the E.D. I presented the different waiting profile data to Nursing, Admitting, Radiology, Respiratory Therapy and Laboratory Services. Whereas each department maintained data on their own performance on admitted patients, no one had demonstrated our admitted-to-hospital patient movement from the front door to the inpatient bed. I submitted a manuscript for publication to a prestigious emergency medicine journal. The descriptive statistical article described the success and faults of our system. The discussion section of the manuscript rendered a comparative analysis of existing data from other institutions. Since no other published studies existed that detailed admissions from a pediatric facility, I was sure of an accepted publication. To my surprise, the manuscript was rejected. The reviewers found the content of the paper acceptable, but they found disfavor with my suggestion that C.H.M.C.'s admitting process should be a model for comparison. They thought publication of such woeful inefficient time management would tarnish the hospital's reputation.

SCHOLARLY PURSUITS

Dr. Peter Rosen, "grandfather of emergency medicine" in the eyes of many, stated at conference I attended, "For the physician employed in an academic center, the publishing zone in their brain must comfortably rest in proximity to their brain's erogenous zone." Peter, who had edited the first textbook devoted to the discipline of Emergency Medicine, implied by this humorous remark that publishing information in some format was an energy-sustaining and rewarding pursuit. Indeed, for medical school faculty members, in order to ascend the academic ladder in their branch of medicine, one of the necessary achievements was publishing.

The academic community, whether on the collegiate or medical school level, believed the single most important and consistent measure of a faculty member's academic worth was publication. Medical schools prized the teacher whose contributions to the diverse body of literature were accepted and printed. Not all printed words had equal weight. The most important words were published in peer-review journals.

There were many peer-review journals in my early faculty days. There were several prominent periodicals, such as *Journal of American Medical Association* or *New England Journal of Medicine,* that published general medical information suitable for any medical audience. They on occasion published an article by an emergency physician. However, emergency physicians found greater pride in publishing in a journal that catered to their specialty. At the time that I submitted my manuscript on admitted patient flow, *Annals of Emergency Medicine* was the only E.M. specialty journal that was "indexed" or officially recognized by the National Library of Medicine.

I sent my manuscript to the editorial offices of *Annals of Emergency Medicine*. They retained an editorial board whose structure was similar to other peer-review journals. The editors maintained a cadre of learned reviewers who consented to form an opinion regarding a submitted manuscript. Reviewers had to commit their thoughts via a structured written report within a few weeks from receipt to a journal sub-editor. Reviewers were asked to accept or reject a manuscript outright or potentially accept a manuscript with revisions that they felt were necessary. If two reviewers agreed, the sub-editor generally concurred and the author was informed of the journal's decision. If the reviewers disagreed, the sub-editor determined the ultimate decision. The sub-editor ultimately provided the message to the authors of acceptance, rejection, or need for amendment and suggested re-submission for further consideration.

Annals of Emergency Medicine, in order to reduce bias like other editorial offices, deleted the author's name and blinded the reviewers to the identity of the physician and institution that sponsored the manuscript. The editorial offices chose reviewers who had typically published on the topic, acquired grant monies to research the area in question, had lectured on the subject, or for other reasons were held as experts by their colleagues. Your potential peers were deemed the best reviewers.

My manuscript describing admission flow patterns was rejected by my peers. Rejection rates at the time for the most prestigious journals were as high as 60-70%. Had there been another suitable journal for my manuscript, I would have amended the information based on reviewer suggestions and sent it elsewhere. By the next decade, three additional emergency medicine journals made the re-submission of rejected manuscripts possible.

THERE'S NO SOUR GRAPES HERE SIRS,
JUST A LESSON FROM AMERICA'S SPORT;
I MUST RELATE THAT YOU MISSED THE CALL.

Perhaps you recall the event, an autumn date
When the Red Machine was in all its glory?
The ump had his posterior to the plate
When he made "The Call" of ignominy.
Incredulous, the Main Spark came runnin'
Each expiration in transit quite audible.
The man with a reputation for his tongue
Gave no lashing; his words were laudable:
"You missed the call, and the tape will show it."
I recall his acceptance of error seemed awkward.
"Epiglottitis at the Extremes of Age" is my manuscript.
Your Editorial Board must have had their rears forward.

In the academic world, even within the realm of peer-reviewed acclaim, not all publications were equal. A publication under your sole authorship cast you in the most favorable light. Where multiple authors contributed to a publication, their credited benefit to those listed behind the second or third author was non-existent. Further, the paper that counted above all other contributions to science was a printed description of original research. Bench research, where discoveries were germinated in test tubes or clinical research that subjected patients to trials, were equal weighted as gold bouillon.

In 1981-82, at the suggestion of Dr. Bill Carroll, an energized third-year pediatric resident, six physicians presented a research proposal to C.H.M..C.'s Institutional Review Board. They accepted our offer to carry out a study on young patients at high risk for serious bacterial infection who presented to C.H.M.C. E.D. Any child between 6-24 months with a temperature greater than or equal to 104 degrees F. who had no apparent focus of infection was eligible for study. After laboratory testing excluded a hidden infection such as pneumonia, urinary tract infection or meningitis, patients with an elevated white blood cell count were eligible for enrollment. The study doctor on call for the day was paged. We approached the parent with the medical information known at the time. We advised the parents that no doctors knew whether giving a shot of penicillin now would help their child. Our intent as part of this study was to gain information on the outcome of their child's illness. If the parent consented, we would randomize (like a game of chance) their child to treatment with a shot or provide no antibiotics depending upon the last number printed on sealed, coded message.

Being within the department on a daily basis, I assumed a major responsibility for securing enrollment and seeing children in daily follow-up. Within the first hours of the study's beginning, I approached a dad who had brought his febrile child in for a shot of penicillin. He felt the injection was necessary to get his child better. I explained our study was designed to determine whether his suggestion was medically sound. He listened intently to me, then responded, "You mean you don't know what to do. You are not 'perimenting on my child!" He turned and fled the room with his child under his wing.

What I thought would be an easy and rapidly-completed study took over a year to complete. We spent another three months revising drafts of the manuscript. We submitted the article to *Pediatrics*, the official journal of the American Academy of Pediatrics. Their reviewers accepted the article. When it was published in 1983, it was the only article that had addressed the medical dilemma of managing a select age group of febrile children without an apparent focus of infection.

The article I published on the management of mouth injuries in *Pediatric Emergency Care* was an example of an in-depth review. Individual case histories were provided to illustrate points and the relevant collective literature was analyzed. Well-written review articles typically provided the historical perspective of respected authorship and stated current assertions. Despite the potential clarity of reviews, they were weighted only slightly above the most inferior peer-reviewed publication, the case report.

A case report was publishable in only several circumstances. The first and most common situation was a unique, or nearly unique event that represented a previously undescribed illness. A unique case that reflected a "new" disease was publishable in any of the medical journals. The emergency journals would publish a case that represented a new and important variation of emergency presentation from the expected pattern. Cases of unexpected events or cases with two or more diseases unexpectedly associated with each other were also publishable.

I failed to report the coagulation disturbance we documented in the two brothers who gave themselves intravenous marijuana. I failed to report the consecutive serious bacterial infection from the same germ in Mary Renae and brother, Christopher. I also let another event slip away.

A three-year-old girl was brought to the E.D. for evaluation of abrupt onset of high fever, sore throat, and refusal to feed. The child appeared anxious and sat bolt upright. She preserved the opening of her air passages by keeping her neck and head stiff. Her mouth hung open, drool slipping from her bottom lip. I suspected the child had a serious infection of a throat structure called an epiglottis. Inflammation of this protective tissue that normally rested silently on top of the wind pipe could rapidly cut off the child's ability to breathe. I explained to the mother that the child would need to have an immediate examination of her air passage, and if infection was confirmed, we would place a tube in her child's windpipe and give antibiotics to treat this life threat. The mother replied, "Oh, you mean direct laryngoscopy and an endotracheal tube. My six-year-old daughter has been in your I.C.U. for three days receiving similar treatment for her epiglottitis." I had never encountered epiglottitis in siblings. When I searched the existing literature, I found no case reports. Before I submitted my manuscript, Dr. Handler from Philadelphia published a case report of epiglottitis in siblings.

What one physician encountered in practice may be a chance occurrence that never will repeat itself in the physician's lifetime, nor will a similar event be seen by another practitioner. However, if a physician reported an unusual event, it was possible that as a direct result of the report, another patient could be accurately diagnosed. A good example was the case report of Dr. Ellen Fishbein, who was a few years ahead of me at C.H.M..C. in her pediatric training. Ellen had performed a routine preoperative physical examination for a child who was to undergo surgical lengthening of his tight heel cords. She noted the child had an unexplained history of sweating and flushing. Ellen found the child to have elevated blood pressure. Ellen delayed surgery and uncovered the presence of an exceedingly rare tumor called pheochromocytoma. The heel cord lengthening and pheochromocytoma may have been an aberrancy but her published case report on pheochromocytoma in a patient with tight heel cords led to this suspicion and ultimate discovery of pheochromocytoma in another child at C.H.M.C. who was to have his heel cords lengthened.

What one physician encountered in practice and reported in the literature may have been seen by a number of practitioners who had not attempted to author a similar manuscript. Upon reading of a previously-thought "unique" case, others with similar cases then committed their experiences to writing. A unique case that had been a twist on a theme then came to be known as a recognized and accepted entity. A good example of this process was my publication in 1979 of several children who had been brought by their parents to the E.D. for lethargy. The children were ultimately discovered to have intussusception, an obstruction of their bowel. I had no explanation for their altered mental status. Dr. Milton Tenenbein, a Canadian, called me after my publication appeared. He had seen the same circumstance. He thought the children's lethargy was a result of elevated blood endorphins, naturally occurring substances produced by our body leading to a soothing effect. Although his study failed to prove endorphins as a mechanism, his manuscript was accepted. Others subsequently submitted intussusception patients with lethargy to other investigations. Ultimately, collective review articles and textbook chapters emphasized altered mental status as a presenting clinical manifestation of intussusception.

The academic community gave little credit to someone who accepted an invitation from an editor to write a textbook chapter. However, medical textbooks have retained their worth over the decades. They have provided summed information in one resource for the medical student, resident in training or practitioner. When well-written, the chapter contained the most current information for the reader. Unfortunately, from the time a chapter was written until the time that a publisher offered the text for purchase, two years passed. The proferred newest information was old news or outdated by new discovery published in peer-review journals. Popular textbooks with brisk sales have therefore been updated with frequency from spans of one to five years.

Despite the lack of academic worth attributed to its production, I was thrilled to be asked to write all of the six pediatric chapters of Dr. Peter Rosen's first edition text, entitled *Emergency Medicine: Concepts and Clinical Practice.* I focused the writing according to the recommended style. I submitted these six new creations in a timely fashion to my sub-editor. I followed his recommendations for minor changes. Ultimately, I was rewarded with a free copy of the book for my significant investment of time.

For the second edition of the text, I was asked to update three of the chapters. Three of my existing chapters were assigned to other authors as the sub-editors wished to increase the authorship within their second edition. For the third edition, my sub-editor restricted me to one chapter on bacterial meningitis. The two others were reassigned.

Like all other authors who submitted a textbook chapter, each time I submitted a chapter I had signed a consent indicating that the publishers had the sole right to my works. I had given away any sense of control of the chapter I had written. The editors and sub-editors had no contractual obligation to engage me in any of the existing writing for future editions. I, like other authors who had been denied authorship, was disappointed by the prospect of a reduced contribution to the literature. Further, I was offended that other authors had utilized 90% of my original contribution. They modified 10% and called the chapter their own in future editons of the text. In an attempt to induce consciosness and consideration of the question "What constitutes authorship?" I submitted the following verse.

EMBATTLED CHAPTERS: CONCEPTS AND PRACTICE

When musketeers, Jones, Brown, Reiley, et al. totalled five
I composed the Selected Pediatric Emergencies section.
Daniel was the swashbuckler who orchestrated my goings-on.
He complimented the timely and introspective
Submission of six "monolithic diatribes."
Wilson's knightliness was a tailored addition
For the next reinforcement of their prestigious text.
However, it was the knave Johns, my neighbor,
Unleashed falconer who skewered my breast:
"Your works are halved" and assigned to other contributors.
Hillman, Walters, Matthew became legionnaires.
What had been twice encased was thrice
Displayed then conjoined in verdant hue.
With force of their brigade in rears, a lone overseer
Unhoused my trilogy and cock-a-doodle-doo!
"Acute Bacterial Meningitis" was but a souvenir.
In ought ninety four, the editorial phalanx
Convened for purposes of planning the ninety six release.
They commissioned foot soldiers to embark
On refreshing my timeworn, but largely valid piece.
Once woo'd, now blinded to cannoneers, I'm cuckolded.
Is this not a lamentable state when your standing
Army of sentences and oft' times paragraphs
Are detached from your breastplate and planning
By conscripts who are your unbidden guests?
Has the concept of authorship been lost in practice?

NON-BEDSIDE TEACHING

A teacher of medicine in the presence of students away from a patient's bedside could provide insights. As a novice educator, I was most comfortable among a small number of learners. With relatively little preparation or anxiety I capably held formal or informal small group discussions. With greater preparation and worry over impact of my words and influence of my style, I routinely addressed classes of 30-50 students. In order to face an audience of 100, I needed several months lead time to review my literature file, seek the newest information from other resources, construct visual aides, practice the delivery, reassess my weaknesses and revise the presentation.

Typical classroom presentations where the professor hugged the podium and dominated the verbal exchange were boring to me as a student. As a teacher, I recognized adult learners needed more active participation and required inclusion in discussions. Practical applications needed to be incorporated to maintain relevance. As an example, it made more sense to me to have students taste various antibiotic suspensions and gag from the repugnant ones than to provide them a written list of the good flavors and the bad.

I attended local teaching sessions of my fellow faculty and selectively traveled to meetings in order to witness teachers with a national reputation. From their examples, I accepted and individualized favorable methods of instruction. I learned to avoid behaviors that were detrimental.

With time others asked me to present at regional or national meetings. I was learned, reflective, humorous and illuminating until I spoke at the Annual Kentucky American Medical Association general meeting. I was ill-prepared to face greater than 1,000 doctors from all disciplines of medicine who reservedly clapped upon hearing my initial roots and lingering tentacles rested north of the Ohio river. Not one smiled at my lead-off story intended to cast humor on the differences in sexual appetites of men and women. My abdomen immediately ached as if I were struck below the belt. I knew that John Buchino, then a pediatric pathologist in Louisville who attended the meeting, was embarrassed by my flat delivery, dry mouth, halting vocalizations. Had he been asked, he would have denied our friendship three times by the cock crow.

Before I sheepishly retreated from the Convention Center Ballroom, the purebred Lexington speaker who followed me reflected as his lead comment on the unnecessary predilection of his stud horse to use ropes when he clearly was on top of the mating situation. The assemblage to a person laughed in unison. From that experience I learned a successful speaker had to know the perversions and bias of his audience.

My most successful hour as an educator resulted from my association with Dr. Glenn C. Hamilton. Glenn was an emergency medicine faculty member at the University of Cincinnati College of Medicine. He was the Educational Coordinator for their residency program. He scheduled and monitored the impact of their residents' didactic sessions and experiential rotations. We met at the conference I sponsored at King's Island Amusement Park entitled, "Screaming Demons and Beasts—The Kid Less than Two in Your E.D." At Glenn's request, I later spoke at a conference he organized on respiratory illnesses in emergency medicine. In between talks, we found ourselves sharing common interests as educators, and equally un-enthralled by our immediate supervisors. Within a year, Glenn became Chairman of the Department of Emergency Medicine at Wright State University School of Medicine in Dayton, Ohio. He retained his residence in Cincinnati, not more than two miles from my home and for a year commuted 50 miles to the office. He took a plane to Cozumel, Mexico at the invitation of EPIC Medical Expeditions who concentrated on continuing medical education in the outdoors. He delivered medical information to emergency physicians in between scuba-diving instruction. He graciously recommended me as a speaker for the same company's sailboat adventure in Hawaii.

I met my audience of seven emergency physicians at dusk, pool side in the old whaling town of Lahaina. We covered one hour worth of the 19-hour syllabus in a relaxed atmosphere before retiring. The next morning, with my feet solidly on the deck, I elevated Ruth by her bottom while the co-captain of our 50' sail boat yanked on her arms. When everyone completed their laughter, we set sail for an eight-day excursion tacking in-between islands. The first night we slept less comfortably than the seven that followed. We quickly learned to retire under sand-filled sheets, unclean to share head space with reserve sails. At sunrise of our second day, my students had requested that I teach no more as it inhibited their sailing. I complied. One week later, we sat on solid land on Lanai around a weathered picnic table. We discussed the post conference test questions. I encouraged circling of the responses guaranteed to secure their successful accreditation for completion of the course.

CHANGING BOSSES

Dr. Mark McGovern had a pleasant teaching style. He took great care of patients, concentrating his efforts on abused and neglected children. He published several novel articles on child abuse. He wasn't consumed by remaining full-time in an academic environment. He retired as my immediate boss to an ambulatory pediatric practice in the suburbs. When we celebrated his going-away luncheon, he took my light-hearted criticism well when I presented him with a blue-print of the hospital's ground floor highlighting the location of the Emergency Department. Although he was responsible for the E.D. as well as the clinics, he had rarely stepped foot in the area he left under my direction.

For over a year, as a quite inexperienced faculty member, I worked without a boss. With the controllers, we slowly implemented change. Movement of a single hallway chair after prolonged debate was tangible proof of progress accomplished by a committee. The impact of levitation was more immediate than our joint decision to pour concrete into the artificial pond outside the hospital's entrance. The shallow circulating pool was a potential venous fly trap to youthful adventurers, who descended head-first for discarded pennies.

There were other physical and emotional advancements in the administration of the E.D., not necessarily from my actions, but as a result of investments made by others. Eventually, a hospital-wide committee was formed to engage more of the professional staff and the private practitioners in decision-making.

The hospital also established a search committee and ultimately hired Dr. Emil Bowden to replace Dr. McGovern. Bowden had in his career faced complex problems in the outpatient department of a small children's hospital. He solved many. On the basis of his actions, he applied the principles to print and was granted respect for his published authorship on administration of an ambulatory department in an academic environment.

Dr. Bowden's thoughts regarding pediatric emergency care at C.H.M.C. were largely sound. His plans for changes seemed appropriate. He was granted a honeymoon period by the controllers and accomplished relative miracles promptly. He felt compelled to offer me his hard-won wisdom. Bowden suggested my previous failures had sprung from three sources. From his unsolicited estimate, I had made a poor social contract with my colleagues. As a result, I had not built an effective health care team. Secondly, I lacked an administrative armentarium. When confronted by a profusion of rules and paradigms, I was maladapted. Last, and most devastatingly, my unwillingness to wear a neck tie despite his insistence proved my lack of professionalism. Since I could not managed myself, the people and the organization could not profit.

Bowden felt I could improve if I watched him and emulated his leadership style. Within a month of his arrival, Bowden's superior collegial discipline evaporated. I was officed next to him and knew he was engaged at the time with Alaine Barsan in a scheduled weekly meeting. I heard the muffled sounds of heated discussion escalate to argument. The explosion of the door slamming signaled the permanent loss of harmonious professional building with nursing. In the short time that followed, Bowden sequentially touched other physician leaders, clerical, admitting, ancillary services and administrative personnel by thoughts, words and actions that laid bare his own self-interest and emphasized open disregard for other's opinions.

I found myself in the humiliated position of following Bowden's directions at the risk of destroying relationships. I more often chose to disregard Bowden's directions, which I interpreted to be abusive edicts that would do little to promote our fragile societal structure in the Emergency Department. He interpreted my unresponsiveness as rebellious, distracting, and disrespectful.

Ultimately, I disavowed myself from Bowden and suspended all contact whenever possible. I had thought he displayed sufficient offending behaviors and attitudes that burdened progress. I anticipated he would be fired. When the distributive justice did not occur, I took the position as the Pediatric Coordinator within the Department of Emergency Medicine at Wright State University located in Dayton, Ohio. I sought the influence of academic emergency physicians who shared my expectations.

ESTABLISHING DEPARTMENTAL PATHS

The well-rooted University of Cincinnati College of Medicine had produced doctors since 1871. The Department of Pediatrics at the university had a well earned reputation for generating and disseminating new knowledge. By various estimates of productivity, it rested in the top 10% of the nation's roughly 150 pediatric departments. The pediatric faculty, with a wide-range depth of expertise, were long noted for stimulating inquisitive pediatric residents and medical students.

The seed for Wright State University School of Medicine was sown in 1974. Interns seeking to deliver responsible, humanistic and competent emergency care were admitted to the Integrated Residency in Emergency Medicine, which was established in 1978. The School of Medicine conferred the highly prized departmental status upon Emergency Medicine in 1980. At the time, there were only four other Emergency Medicine Departments in the United States. None of the peer group had yet commanded greater attention, although all aspired to excellence.

Over Dr. Hamilton's door hung the framed philosophy written more than a century ago by Louis Pasteur: "Fortune smiles on the mind that is prepared to receive her gifts." My new boss possessed a self-confident, active mind. He met with the assembled earliest faculty for no less than three hours weekly. We attempted to map our potential relationships with the community, the university and the medical school. Ultimately, we defined the essential components of a quality Emergency Medicine Department. We determined that teaching, research and service were our pathways toward success.

Since there was little history and the relative absence of models to emulate, we were fundamentally creating a group blueprint. Not every faculty member had equal architectural skills, yet we persisted. By our nature, we had gravitated to a medical specialty that clinically required prompt decision-making and fluidity. We were unaccustomed to unraveling all the facts, weighing the relative worth of each variable and structuring short and long term, innovative strategies.

INDIVIDUAL FACULTY DEVELOPMENT

Dr. Hamilton demanded that we gave appropriate attention toward our own personal development. He extracted our individual goals and objectives. Each autumn we committed our plans to writing, and at a full retreat we highlighted our outlines. At these meetings, we pushed each other to grow professionally and interpersonally.

As part of our ongoing faculty development, on a yearly basis we were instructed to update our curriculum vitae.

THE FUTILITY OF AN ACADEMIC BLUEPRINT FOR THE NEW YEAR

We oblige our Chairs by revising the personal profile
Of valued, professional lives; or vitae, the curriculum
We originally prepared from sample templates to beguile
An Admissions Committee, certain Directors or a Consortium.
Now on a yearly basis, we update our academic prowess.
Collated, the information is forwarded through the Dean
To the University's Trustees, where effusiveness
Is restrained by repetition and a Governor's overseein'.
CVs attest and proclaim all that is noble on a placard;
We extol the virtues of funded grants and indirects.
MDs highlight the narrow-circle stature from honors and awards
And artfully repress their self-nomination, unvexed.
First-authored text, reviews, and case reports are accolades.
Abstracts, editorials, and invited commentaries are subservient
To peer-accepted works more prominently displayed.

**Unfortunately, the testament is but false wonderment.
The yearly missal we construct too closely resembles
The word-processed Holiday Greetings bulk-mailed
By well-meaning colleagues, whose intentions are credible
But their prose is a missile, that our senses, impales.
We all travel with family for presentations before a host.
Our children are immeasurably gifted, thriving on adoration!
Terminal wishes for a New Year are dwarfed by boasts
Throughout that recast standards of self-congratulation.
The faith community and neighbors gauge the value
Of our earthly passage, not by the titles we avow.
The validity of our science is a dispute they'll eschew
As long as we mend the infirm and spiritually arouse.
If at life's end other physicians render a decree
Regarding academic merit, what is worthy to celebrate,
Enthusiasm for student-centered teaching and humanistic dictate,
Can neither be assayed nor conveyed within a CV.**

Reprinted with permission from *Academic Emergency Medicine* 2:1033, 1995

MEASURING SUCCESS

Dr. John B. McCabe completed his emergency medicine residency at Wright State University and joined the faculty. At our fall retreats over the years he committed to completing and publishing multiple bench research projects. He intended to participate in the Ohio Chapter of the American College of Emergency Physicians (A.C.E.P.) and advance within its structure before participating more fully on the national level. He would then be elected as president of the organization, housed in Texas. He would be chosen as the U.S. editor for an international scientific periodical. He would become the chairman of an Emergency Medicine Department and establish a residency training program.

Each spring the faculty would attend another retreat geared in part to relationship building. An onerous portion of the agenda was to pull out the autumn's goals and objectives and reflect on our individual progress. Most of us confessed to our marginal success. John McCabe required no apologetic reassurances. He published his research in peer-review journals. He became the American editor of *Resuscitation*. He steadily rose among the ranks in A.C.E.P. We both presented papers at the First International Conference in Emergency Medicine held in London, England. While Ruth, John's wife Bonnie and I remained stationery one evening in our formal wear, I watched John glad-hand over 500 occupants of a ballroom. It struck me that he possessed the political expertise and had established sufficient alliances to be elected President of A.C.E.P. Indeed, he assumed that position during the organization's 25th anniversary. I sent him the following poem as a tribute:

THE FELLOW'S INDUCTION

Since inception we've been the frontline support
For ill and injured who've patiently cued at triage.
Educational diversity displayed among marginal resources
Characterized the outliers who crafted our specialty.
As shepherds, they codified in the form of a College
Political, social values and an educational mission.
Pioneers impassioned in debate paid homage
To laudable care by those schooled in a curriculum.
At this 25th assemblage, a limitless reservoir
Of goodwill should prevail, and the resplendent
Inductees recall in one moment of penitence:
Irrevocable is His decision to admit or discharge.

With an immense pride, I was in the audience when John hosted his first ceremony. I was in awe that a person whose social contract involved washing down Pepi's luncheon special with DosEquis beer with me on a bi-monthly basis shared the podium with David Brinkley. When

John left our faculty to chair a department, he established an emergency medicine residency, completing his collective goals.

AN UNCOMMON MAN (Beep, Beep)

I had an appreciative trust and admiration for others among our earliest faculty, especially Dr. Fred Epstein. Fred was another animated University of Cincinnati product Dr. Hamilton recruited. Like me, Fred retained his residence in Cincinnati, forcing a 50-mile commute to the Dayton office. I drove a low-end Volvo within the conservative range of 69-71 MPH to and fro on a 65 MPH limit interstate. I left the Dayton office 15 minutes before Fred. I'd travel almost halfway home, typically reaching the northern outskirts of Middletown, Ohio when I'd capture the sleek frontage of Fred's black Trans Am in my rear view mirror. Within moments, he passed with such velocity that I felt immobile, like Wile E. Coyote watching my elusive highway traversing prey. Intuitively, I knew from the rapid disappearance of Fred's road-running brake lights that he exceeded 100 MPH. With every passage, I mentally employed the algebraic expressions to define an answer to the question, "How fast was Fred going?" I never completed the equation.

Fred was more facile than I with math. At an early November faculty meeting, Fred utilized a chalkboard to illuminate his calculations. He had determined with precise scientific methodology the odds of being assigned his year end Emergency Department shift assignments. He proclaimed with clarity that his schedule for clinical care approximated one in sixteen billion based on chance alone. He had no daytime shifts or shifts during the week. Further, he was positioned in the Emergency Department consecutively on December 24th through December 26th to be freed from clinical duties until the 3 PM-11 PM shift on New Year's Eve. A common man would have suggested the poor fitting schedule strained the credibility of fairness. Fred was content to find the humor in the situation.

Fred's uncommon abilities with math were matched by his command of language. Irrespective of the topic of discussion, an audience was mesmerized by Fred's clarity. He held your attention with phrases unspoken by the general populous. In informal speech, he painted word pictures with a comedic tongue. From the podium, he was a lyricist. He broke hard-to-grasp concepts into components and arranged obtuse material into understandable scenes. His medical parables were not only theatrical, but his language transfixing.

Fred's wife was an Air Force OB-Gyn physician. She was reassigned from Dayton's Wright Patterson Air Force Base to the Eglin Air Force Base in Florida. There were no academic sanctuaries in the panhandle. Fred took over the leadership of a community E.D. in Panama City. Despite his departure from academics, he was retained as a national speaker for A.C.E.P. and continued to publish in the emergency medicine literature.

DOCTOR OF A DIFFERENT KIND

Dr. Jim Olson received his doctorate (Ph.D.) in physiology from Cornell University. His professional interest of uncovering brain mysteries was consonant with the mission of our department. He joined us from the University of California, Berkley as a young investigator. Within a month of his arrival, he demonstrated slide photos of his California projects. With the aid of federal grant dollars, he had manufactured a fashionable jacket with matching helmet that fit the average young lab mouse. He created a miniature glass dome that rested between a fixed monitoring base and a small but high-intensity floodlight. Jim subjected his prey to uninvited restraint within the housing, then flipped the light switch, causing a rapid rise in body temperature. Jim gathered data from the superheated mice and from the microscopic sections of their brain, he postulated on the genesis of seizures from temperature elevation in children.

In his years with us, Dr. Olson invented and refined a method of raising mice brain cells in a petri dish. Other researchers around the world adopted his methods. He and others have since subjected the cultured cells to various insults in order to discern what makes brains swell with various human disease states. He hasn't tired of this pursuit in the two decades we have been together.

Although Jim played softball with no greater skill compared to the weekend warrior M.D.s, he was definitely smarter. Jim and Pam's expectations for their children's mental prowess were also greater. Having a few more years of parental experience and a pediatric background, Jim asked me in the late 1980's the likely cause of his four-year-old's stuttering. Apparently, the child's aberrant speech pattern was most noticeable when he was confined in their "Learning Chair." Upon further inquiry, I understood each child spent designated periods of time in the seat. The sole purpose of the seat was to magnify the child's pursuit of knowledge over a wide ranging field. With advancing age, the skills required in the Learning Chair intensified. I believe there were no floodlights, and I don't think the kids were physically strapped in place, but I did suggest to Jim that most parents utilized a similar technique. However, the "Time Out" chair was generally perceived as punishment. Their oldest child's speech was normal long before he entered Harvard University.

OTHER BENCH AND CLINICAL RESEARCHERS

Dr. John Lyman was among the first scientists who uncovered man's biological rhythms. As a young investigator, he imprisoned volunteers within a clock-less setting where subjects could not determine by any external clues the actual time of day. He watched their awake and sleep patterns to discover we had internal clocks. Subsequently, industries that subject workers to changing shifts, including emergency medicine workers, used John's data to improve emotional well-being and performance effectiveness. John's legacy, however, emanates from his experiment with me in 1983. By inviting me to join him in a game of Hangman on a screen, he induced me to strike the "Enter" key. This was an error on my part, as I had previously decided my epitaph would read, "Here lies Singer; the man never touched the computer." It would be 15 years before I again manipulated the keyboard.

Dr. Mark Angelos was interested in devices, techniques and drugs that could be applied to patients whose hearts stopped as a result of a heart attack. In order to gather information on the strength of blood flow within the heart, he mechanically created an identical heart attack in multiple dogs. Each dog was subjected to a different resuscitative technique. The data was analyzed and conclusions provided to audiences at emergency medicine meetings and to readers of his publications.

Mark's professional activity and the intermittent barking from the basement of our office building brought attention from animal rights activists. They and faculty members from other emergency medicine departments around the country sought Mark for opposing reasons. Mark ultimately vacated our subterranean canine I.C.U. when he transferred to the Ohio State University's Department of Emergency Medicine. The move permitted Mark greater time with his ever-enlarging family.

*** SEEKING AN ACADEMICALLY-ORIENTED PHYSICIAN**

Those of us (old and familiar) who have been islanded
At one or two institutions of post-grad education
For a quarter century consciously vitalizing the young
Are periodically convulsed by a well-penned
Wholly reflective, rueful letter of resignation.
Repetitiously we grieve, rejoice, and worry
For an office mate who evokes pleasurable acclamation.
We'll post a notice* while our embrace is affectional;
The melancholy will hold a wake, through none's buried.
Hey, will there be anyone left to attend my "funeral"?

Reprinted with permission from *Academic Emergency Medicine* 3:871,1996

Clif Sheets' first research was an outgrowth of his interest in microbiology. As a college student, he combined his love for wildlife and water craft with scientific pursuit to explore infectious diseases encountered with marine life. At a faculty meeting, he revealed slides of his early adventures. Clif, a gentle giant of a man, dwarfed all other sailors viewed on board any research vessel. Clif's large brain was proportionate to his body but disproportionately engaged.

Dr. Clif Sheets was multi-talented. He demonstrated brilliance in patient care and in organizational finesse in his teaching. In an unforgettable informal hour of instruction to an audience of 40 physicians, Clif presented his successful method of recalling medical information through word association. Without difficulty, he had the capacity to spontaneously recall and deliver in correct order a complete list from various figures contained in an emergency medicine text. With a little practice, I witnessed Clif impress a larger audience. At a departmental Christmas party held at the Hamilton home, Clif was one of three who floored us with seasonal tunes. The notes reached by the trumpet, trombone and french horns of Drs. Sheets, Hamilton and Khromer caused me to fling a quarter toward their feet at an invisible collection basket. The mischievous action invoked more laughter than my opening prayer.

PLEASANT TIE OF HOST & GUEST

O Lord, grant through your infinite powers
That those who lie in life's sweet sunset
Be pedestaled by genial breeze
On earth, for at least another week.
For they, like us, with unfaltering trust
Are eager to celebrate the natal day.
Father, may you brighten the eyes of all
Entwined by the pleasant tie of host and guest
Who gather, as we, in simple fellowship.
We ask for provision of a balanced soul
As we eddy, raptured, spent on food and drink.
Please don't let us trash the Hamilton's house.

TANGIBLE REWARDS OF ENTHUSIASM

My Wright State faculty colleagues strove to improve the database of our medical students. They searched and experimented to ultimately adjust customary ways of teaching from the lectern and the bedside. Collectively, we used the whole of our talent, and our deeds were amply rewarded.

In my fourth year of teaching, a junior medical student spontaneously sent me a brief note that made me walk thereafter more upright. She complimented my delivery of an improved emergency medicine course to her classmates. She praised my energy and organizational creativity. She indicated that my apparent teaching mission led to my nomination for their class's year-ending faculty teaching award. Another educator had ultimately crossed the threshold before me, but she wanted to thank me nevertheless. Her hint of near-communal enjoyment of excellence created a reservoir of warmth and sustained productivity. Two years later, I was nominated and named as the award winner.

Dr. Timothy Janz, who had trained in emergency medicine and in critical care, joined our department during the first epic of faculty expansion. Over the years, his genuine teaching wealth was distributed to more than 1000 students. Tim received their prestigious teaching medal on three occasions.

OVERCOMING DILEMMAS

All of us were comfortable delivering high-quality medical care to the infirm who presented for treatment in the E.D. It was less energy-consuming to independently see patients than it was to oversee the care delivered by the students and residents.

Preceptorship was conceptually manageable. We were to assure prompt service and provide instant illumination for the learner on the topic pertinent to their patient's provisional diagnosis. When the volume and acuity were constant, we were a shoreline that could satisfy both the consumer and the student. However, waves of battlement were not uncommon. More than a single critically ill patient or severely traumatized individual concurrent with the normal magnitude of infirmities could dissolve the steady state of the teacher providing patient care.

The provision of supervisory education was driven by logic. When we were woefully behind and patients were waiting several hours to see a physician, I and others abbreviated the teaching. When we extinguished long waits, we resumed teaching.

The provision of a faculty member's supervisory care was also driven by logic. For the novice, we had to provide greater oversight and even be repetitive in our history-taking or physical examinations in order to assure safe judgment. For those students and residents who had firmly anchored clinical skills, we granted more autonomy.

Dilemmas still occurred. The best outcome for a critically ill or injured patient would likely rest in the hands of the most capable, yet the less capable would profit most from the challenge. As supervisors, we had to promptly weigh the potential merits and deficits of an assignment and distribute the work to everyone's benefit.

On occasion, logic could not drive action, and infrequent experience could not clarify direction. Two similar cases provide example.

A three-year-old received an injection of an antibiotic at his doctor's office for an infected throat. On the way home, his mother first noted intense redness on her child's face. Within moments, her child's lips swelled enormously. She deviated from her path home to the Emergency Department. On arrival, it was apparent that the child was in the midst of anaphylaxis, a potentially lethal allergic reaction. I called for the appropriate medical management but the left the child's side in order to retrieve my camera. The need to preserve the child's characteristic facial findings as a future educational tool drove me to temporary abandonment. As an afterthought, I convinced myself that my actions were merited. A second encounter has made me ambivalent.

An eight-year-old girl without any recognized medical problems went trick-or-treating with her supervising mother. Without warning, while traversing a neighbor's front yard, the child gently lost control of her body. From the car, the mother witnessed no injury. When she got to her child's side, the mother noted uncontrolled twitching of the girl's right face and right arm. A life squad brought the girl to our Emergency Department. I recognized that the child suffered from a focal motor seizure. There was no impairment of her vital signs and no difficulty with her breathing. I promptly considered there was no deterrent to capturing a once-in-a-lifetime photo that depicted a rightward- fixed-gazing, multicolored spiked-haired individual with rhythmic contractions. The arresting picture remains in my collection. More than imaginary goblins now haunt me on Halloween Eves.

VIOLATING OATHS

My audible oaths that constituted formal prayers subsided exponentially after the death of maternal grandfather, Israel Rukin, when I was in kindergarten. In elementary school, as an elected student counselor, I verbally pledged allegiance to the flag. I participated in the oath well beyond the insertion of "under God." Since elementary school, the only other times that I have invoked His name have been in poetry or in silent intentions. By high school, the highest civil office I held was home room representation for the Red Cross. Our only pledges were monetary. So it was not unusual, that at our medical school graduation, I did not utter out loud the Hippocratic Oath in unison with my classmates.

The original Hippocratic Oath stipulated that as a healer, physicians conduct themselves morally. Over centuries, evolutionary changes were imposed by various medical institutions. Our specific modernized pledge retained the concept of human healing, practiced by people dedicated to the exercise of highest morals. Although I never uttered the words, I concurred with the thoughts. Unfortunately, the message failed at a later date to illuminate behaviors in circumstances involving an interpreter or a gracefully tattooed woman.

Our E.D. maintained a list of adults who willingly served as interpreters. Our staff successfully contacted a woman who volunteered to leave her place of employment to aid my communication with a Chinese child with abdominal complaints. The child carried prescribed pharmaceuticals in two containers labeled with Chinese symbols. Without the interpreter's assistance, I would have been unable to address the child's apparent exacerbation of underlying esophagitis, intensified by consumption of consecutive super-sized McDonald's meals. The history and physical exam consumed ten minutes, but I spent an equal length of time pursuing the interpreter's educational route and professional pursuits. An emergency medicine resident, noting my perplexed appearance sitting at the dictation station, inquired if I was uncertain of the necessary medical path to take with my patient. I replied, "The Hippocratic Oath suggests advances toward a vulnerable patient are forbidden. Likewise, one cannot exhibit provacative behaviors toward the patient's parent or other family member. But has the Oath addressed hitting on an interpreter of a patient? I am captured by ambiguity."

He laughed and then responded from his perspective.

"There is no such onerous restriction that I recall," at which point an adjacent colleague stated the point was moot since I was married.

On a summer's day, I was seeing patients in our Fast Track. A first-time mom brought her three-week-old son for complaints of constipation. He would not eliminate his bowels unless his rectum was stimulated by a suppository. I estimated the mother was in her early 20's. She wore a fashionable, wide-rimmed, leather hat from which a singular wisp of tightly-curled brunette hair rested across a manicured brow. A magnificent tattoo was partially visible under the thin varnish of her elastic halter top. An American flag was unfurled on the superior aspect of her left breast. In repeated snapshot views, I saw the rectangular symbol was the background for the word "Harley." The less apparent title "Davidson" disappeared toward a prominent areola. A red rose rested in the center of an oval frame under her right scapula. The fiction of prophetic truth surrounding the budding arrangement read, "Property of Phil."

I told the mother that I was confident of the child's status of good health. However, I wanted to share the case with one of my colleagues working in the main Emergency Department. Dr. Marcus Bailey, I explained, was a pediatric emergency physician like myself, but he had an additional year of neonatology fellowship where he cared exclusively for children with problems incurred in the first month of life. She consented, and I got the message to Marcus that I requested his consultation. He liberated Dr. Donald Raymon, the concurrently working pediatric emergency physician. When they arrived, I introduced them to the mother and the child's chief complaint of constipation. After less than two minutes, Marcus encouraged me to exit the room so he could transfer his thoughts. Marcus grabbed my arm, moved me out of the reach of her hearing and consumed by the thought, he exploded in laughter. He thanked me for sharing more than the woman's frail ringlet. Donald exited shortly thereafter and in furrowed brow conveyed the case was not infantile botulism, neonatal hypothyroidism or Hirschsprung's disease. He felt constipation to be likely related to formula intolerance. Only Marcus understood my smudging of the Hippocratic Oath.

TAKING INVENTORY

In the cases depicted above, I bent the set of values, attitudes and behaviors that had been established by my physician predecessors. For centuries, we have been trusted by society to uphold the primacy of our service mission. We were pledged to suspend our self-interests. The grounded professional served the interests of patients and society before his own. My misdeeds were not worthy of respect. I had erred. These were circumstances of selective dishonesty and intermittent integrity. Yet they reflected lifelong partial application of ethical principles. At least I had the insight to admit imperfection.

When an opportunity arose to expertly inventory the status of my professionalism, I took advantage of departmental financial support to attend a week-long seminar offered by a group of senior medical educators, psychologists and social workers.

After the students and teachers exchanged introductory remarks within a college classroom, we were shepherded outdoors for play under a welcomed California January sunshine. We divided into teams to engage in traditional picnic-enhancing activities such as volleyball, badminton and Nerf baseball. After athletics, the 30 of us were amassed within 20 square feet, blindfolded and tied together by clothesline. We were alternately provided with riddles or requested to follow explicit instructions. At the end of the day, we welcomed a shower, completed a communal dinner, and then were exposed to videotapes of our previous four hours together. The two hours of discussion that followed centered on highlights of what I had earlier considered to be play. The freeze-framed documentary with professional commentary provided the most illuminating analysis I've ever occasioned. The faculty had memorialized human interactional skills. The compassionate assumed the most effective managerial roles. The caring were the most effective motivators. The sensitive accomplished conflict management. Intellect won out for problem solution, but refinement of character resulted in progress. Those periodically oriented to self-promotion blushed at their obvious diminished worth. Fatigued at the time zone change, I nevertheless reclined sleepless that night, resurrecting the day. The faculty with other nontraditional exercises helped me critically appraise my humanistic orientation.

Emphasis on self-appraisal was a powerful source for change, but like others in advance of the course, I was conveniently blind to performance as evaluated by observations of others. Through the use of psychological measurements, I had the opportunity to estimate the reliability of other's observations by measuring agreement between various observers.

Before the journey west, I answered a lengthy survey. I recorded my student-centered instruction strategy and my preceptorship attitude toward teaching. I committed to circling multiple responses that assessed my reliance on applied problem solving and my humanistic orientation toward my supervisor, colleagues of equivalent rank, and those subservient to me in a professional role. Dr. Hamilton, four academic faculty members, and two secretaries within the department answered a similar questionnaire. The surveys were graded by our instructors. At the conference, all of the attendants received personalized feedback.

I had recognized and acknowledged many of my faults. The deficits included fear of unanticipated obstacles, withdrawal in the face of uncertainty, unwillingness to face detractors, inability to set limits and control others.

Despite my assertions to the contrary, my colleagues felt I was unable to consistently identify, analyze and solve problems. My colleagues felt I could not always be relied upon to use sound judgement. They felt I could be mislead by a seductive hypothesis.

KNOW WHERE TO LOOK?

It must have been the black man.
Cause I know it weren't my brother.
He wouldn't have sold his skin
For a soiled forty dollar.
Two twenties, they was sittin' there
Just askin' to be taken.
And now they's took?
Know where to look
To find the black children?

By their survey instrument, they confirmed that I did not consider all factors before making decisions. Further, I could not be uniformly relied upon to make decisions that supported the university, and departmental policies and objectives. To my consternation, I had underestimated the impact of my oral and written communication. My colleagues suggested that only on rare occasion was I explicitly clear, concise or logical. More often, I was confusingly tangential, and when in a particularly buoyant mood, obtuse to the point of distraction.

To my credit, in many aspects of my professional life, I had mutual favorable opinions with my superiors, co-equals and subservients. My work was accurate, complete, appropriately organized, and my output was extraordinarily high, far exceeding everyone's expectations. I possessed sufficient knowledge to carry out existing requirements under my job title. We all felt that in my existing roles within the department, I had initiated little, but completed every requested project or task I was assigned. I was remarkably reliable and productive in the face of anyone's challenge.

To my everlasting surprise, my colleagues felt that I treated others impartially, without regard to their professional status or personal attributes. I had earned their trust and respect for maintenance of my supportive working relationships. Indeed, when the instructors constructed our profiles on a character grid, my cross hatches were maximally distant from the co-conspirators, Mussolini and Hitler. My attributes were nearly synonymous, ½ inch off the character traits attributed to Jesus Christ.

BOSS ALSO TO CALIFORNIA

Wright State University sought self-awareness among their faculty as one means of improvement. Another methodology for growth was a sabbatical. A professor sought permission to leave a routine at the university to gain new knowledge at another institution. If granted, the professor expanded a knowledge base and the home university became the ultimate beneficiary of the professor's new skills.

In Dr. Hamilton's seventh year at Wright State University, his application for a sabbatical was approved by the medical school. They blessed his enrollment at Stanford University to gain a Master's Degree in Management. The Dean of the medical school projected Glenn would have enhanced capacity to provide leadership to the medical school. Glenn projected that he would have improved capacity to lead our department. Both parties more than fulfilled their projections, but the year of Glenn's absence was somewhat tumultuous.

Dr. Hamilton asked that I assume the position of Acting Departmental Chairman. I accepted, knowing that the responsibilities would be challenging. I was required to oversee all of the department's faculty and support staff. I was responsible to negotiate and secure adequate financial commitment to direct and supervise a highly competitive, community based residency in emergency medicine, support faculty development, support scholarly research, and maintain partnership with the community making efforts to facilitate the university's mission statement.

Glenn's multi-tasking behaviors were facilitated by an administrative secretary. She devoted all her energies to maximize his effectiveness. She accomplished these tasks within a territory that was larger than my office space. Her foothold served as the anti-room to the palatial square footage of Dr. Hamilton's office. Glenn convinced me to vacate my office and assume his office for the year. He suggested the physical move would improve my efficiency. Emotionally, my altered position would symbolically reflect the change in power.

When I soon occupied the boss's throne, I sensed no electrifying authority. However, the feel was elevating. His chair rested on a laminate plate and a soft pillow ballooned my height over the desk top. Within a week the pillow remolded to the smaller cast of my buttocks.

Within another week, I luncheoned, returned to the solitude of customized comfort and lifted my left buttock ever so slightly. What I had contemplated to be a modest, gaseous emission was surprisingly liquid. I drenched a localized segment of my underwear. Though I precipitously realized the misplaced commentary on the state of the world, I also recognized the immediate need to promptly dry clean my dress pants. I retreated home. All the while, I wondered the impact of leaving the small but perceptible stain on the pillow uncleansed.

GOING WITH THE CASH FLOW

Having defecated on Dr. Hamilton's pillow, the hospital that served as our fiscal agent symbolically returned the favor. In September, they ran into a "transient" budgetary crisis. They closed down several ambulatory services, contracted the physical therapy and respiratory therapy departments. They let go of several middle managers and offered early retirement to personnel who did not have direct patient contact. The remaining administrators froze two of our departmental accounts. The fiscal group that had become my new controllers prohibited transfer of dollars between budget pools. The impact was an immediate and unfortunately nine-month sustained reduction of $9,000 from a $25,000 discretionary sum.

Our capacity to "purchase services" was curtailed until July. From this column we had historically paid a token stipend for professors who visited to speak at our request and reimbursed their travel expenses. The dollars for donuts or prepared sandwiches disappeared for any of the working meetings that typically came at a monthly frequency. The withdrawals from visiting speakers and fueling impetus at committee functions were distracting, but not deleterious.

The Alumni dinner, Christmas party and graduation dinners consumed up to $ 15,000 yearly. The Alumni dinner was held in a private banquet setting somewhere in the city that hosted the American College of Emergency Physician's Scientific Assembly. All current faculty and residents who attended the annual educational seminar on a designated evening joined alumni of the residency for drinks and a dinner. When Dr. Hamilton hosted the first of these autumnal celebrations in 1982, all three of the first graduating class of 1981 attended. The percentage of attendance in subsequent years dropped but each year the alumni pool grew. When more graduates attended to raise glasses among a group with common heritage, the cost exponentially increased.

A COMMUNAL TOAST

The retrieval of information following a clasped hand
Or languishing embrace may be falsely tempered
By field tested responses of a collected alderman.
You need not fear we compare how you adhere
To the advertised praise the night you were commissioned.
We are not here to measure health and happiness;
None have surveyed your assets or bequested accreditation.
The intent of this annual pilgrimage is festiveness!
Raise glasses to heights of a Sequoia, unfurled.
Seek countenances from a mural with common heritance.
From these spirits summon flattering remembrance
Of times past and redeem, with me, unperishing pleasure.

In the year of the sabbatical, a host of attendants returned to celebrate our commonality. Like migratory birds without cautionary need, fifty some individuals were drawn together in the upstairs of a Georgetown eating establishment where Ron, a piano bar singer, magnificently entertained our pilgrims.

HOSTING A SWEET RETURN

Back home there's an explosion of color
As both light and warmth are drawn
Without mystery from day by shortening day.
All but this segment of the country
Forages in preparation of sleep and dream.
Here, there's a constant lake–bottom meal
Of succulents, hearts of palm with vinegarette.
Happily we return to celebrate our commonality.
Like migratory birds without cautionary need
In somewhat more random an assemblage
We're drawn together with expanding pleasure
Seeking your blessing of us, WSU pilgrims.

I was choked with expanding pleasure from our 1989 Alumni dinner until the waitress presented me with the bill for $3,700. I fumbled attempting to calculate the tip. I choked knowing that by October we had all but depleted the purchase service account required for Christmas and graduation celebrations.

When Dr. Hamilton had been present and when he would return, my fiduciary responsibilities for the Alumni dinner were exchanged for verse. I produced a table decoration with an invocation or poem when our party was held within the body of an establishment's main dining area. If we were segregated into our own party room, as in the Hotel del Coronado, I raised a presidential toast.

PRESIDENTIAL TOAST

Received in the arm of Victorian splendor
Surrounded by accoutrements of the day
We're unlikely to ask if the varnished woods
Are supported by any architectural decay,

We too, were blueprinted an exacting path.
You were our mortarboard, truss and rafter.
Looking stalwart long after our relationship
None here seek social cracks in your belvedere.
The mortise of the evening for residents and relics
Alike, shall be impeachable fib, not confession.
Let liquor be the lacquer for our moldings.
The timbers won't rot if we all deny, deny, deny.

The service I performed for the Christmas party in 1989 has not been repeated. Following our Alumni dinner, Ruth and I prepared and froze a large assortment of finger foods. We recruited our friends, the Nurres. In formal attire at our house, Dan and Gail served drinks. Their children, Doug, Dave, Cheryl, and Julie, along with my three children parked cars, checked coats, served hors d'oeuvres and helped clean holiday greetings that had fallen from table tops to floors. After everyone departed, our damage detail noted someone heavy wearing spiked heels obviously stood for a prolonged period in one corner of our dining room. She impaled a segment of flooring like a tinsmith multiple times.

Ruth and I had to deploy the damage management team during the only other holiday party we had hosted. During our celebration of the new year, 1973, I caught three fellow interns smoking marijuana in our kitchen. We rapidly extinguished the flames and vented our anxiety. Our city's police department had a month earlier uncovered a grow light enhanced crop of marijuana in a first year pediatric resident's apartment. After the 1 AM police raid, they handcuffed Eric while he was working a graveyard shift in the pediatric emergency department. Eric was summarily dismissed from the residency and ultimately lost the license to practice medicine in the state.

By June of 1990, we had grown accustomed to finding cheap, legal means for departmental celebrations. However, the graduation had to be held in a formal dining area. We were able to pay for a buffet dinner with the kind financial contributions of six emergency department groups with whom our residents and faculty worked. For the first and last time in our history, the drinks were at the expense of the revelers.

The impact of the cash bar was soporific.

FULFILLING ANOTHER TITLE

Besides functioning as acting chair, Dr. Hamilton asked that I assume the role as program director for the residency. As such, I was to function as the source of vision for the emergency medicine residency. I had to participate in institutional policy making, maintain dialogue with our accreditation bodies and maintain suitable relationships with various administrative bodies. Most importantly, I had to lead our departmental recruitment efforts for residents. As such, I had to screen all incoming applications, and with secretarial staff support, schedule interviews.

In order to secure a high-quality entering class of eight interns, I reviewed the paper documents of 400-500 applicants. The faculty and I interviewed 80. With input from the faculty and existing residents we spent over two hours constructing a rank order list of our top choices. After we had ranked the 30th choice for our ultimate match list, we fatigued. Knowing that the lowest ranked candidate we had previously matched in our program was 26th on our list, we provided no further names from the lesser sought after but still qualified candidates. This arrogance cost me dearly within a two-month time frame.

At 10 AM, the day before the official match list was released to all medical students and all residencies, we were informed that two of our eight positions were unfilled. At noon we were able to take inquiries from any students around the country who were unmatched in emergency medicine. My fellow faculty wished me luck during "the scramble" and went to lunch. I was deprived of sustenance, fixed at Dr. Hamilton's desk, trying again not to soil my pants. I desperately needed to determine what if any negative attributes prevented these unmatched candidates from securing a position. After hours of painful, verbal exchange and faxes, I secured two additional residents. Both had interviewed with us but were in our lower, non-ranked pool. The first was a well-educated and traveled candidate with expertise in the treatment of blood vessel disorders. The second was an amiable, laid-back New Englander. We were worried of the former's capacity to interact with peers and the latter's slovenliness. Before the intellect's tenure was complete, our concerns were manifest. He had been physically pummeled by one of his classmates in a trauma room when an argument over management issues could not be amicably resolved. Our eastern friend raised very young children and a parrot in hospital-owned housing. From the ultimate destruction of the rented residence, more than the bird roamed freely without diapers.

I had contacted Glenn in California before I submitted the rank list. He too saw little need for me to rank beyond the 26th position. We both matured from the impact of not filling. In subsequent years, I submitted a match list with close to 80 candidates. Year by year Glenn and I smiled knowingly as other institutions, often prestigious in the eyes of the most ardent detractor, that were unmatched, filling only after a scramble.

A DECADE SOMEWHAT DISSIMILAR

When Glenn returned, my reward for frugal and inventive behaviors was being named as vice-chair of the department. I was directly responsible to the chair and assumed functions of the chair in the chair's absence.

I was retained for another nine years as program director. I carried out the responsibilities of annually reviewing our potential resident talent in much the same fashion over the decade. When the match process changed from a paper system to the Electronic Residency Application System (E.R.A.S.), I had to alter my process of manual review of hundreds of pounds of collated files stored in cardboard boxes. I was forced to utilize a computer for something other than a game of Hangman.

ANOTHER ERA PASSES

The ragman who brought horse and buggy
Up the cobbled road of my youth
Was the last remnant of my parents' era.

They had accepted the transition from iceman
To Westinghouse and Fuller's workforce redirected.
For me, the main street featured Clyde's
With phosphates, marble counter and glass-enclosed candy.
Marmer sold homemade goods next to Ted's Apothecary.
Twenty years later when med school consumed
My attentions, I overlooked the "super" market
That drove Rizzo's fruit truck out of business.
All the while, beyond my world, binary digits
Bauds, bits and bytes begot cursors and mice.
Medicine was flooded with primers; end-using
Clinicians in EM were told microcomputer uses.[1]
For two additional decades, I've resisted change.
I've held onto mental cross-reference and manilla folders
Worshiping growing xeroxed stacks and unfiled reprints.
Today, I resent this ERAS keyboard I must stroke.

REFERENCE:
1. McCabe JB, McCabe BH. Microcomputer -based filing system for emergency medicine literature. Ann Emerg Med. 1981; 10:87-90.
Reprinted with persmission from *Academic Emergency Medicine* 5:251, 1998

PICKING THE LITTER FROM AN ESSAY

Candidates for residency during both the paper-driven system and the electronic version were required to write a personal statement. An emergency medicine faculty member based in Connecticut wrote an instructional book for students seeking residency. One of the chapters dealt with the construction of a personal statement.

If the author of a personal statement deviated as little as possible from a patented essay, the candidate provided an enduring speech that invoked no criticism. Unfortunately, such essays revealed no sign posts of wisdom and granted no insight into personal attributes. Those who made minor adjustments to the customary prose appeared less aggrandized, but more likeable. Those who only loosely followed structured authority were free to illuminate. The irreverent, who ignored instruction, were both amusing and introspective. The literate, with expansive vision were creative. The penetrative artistry of a few authors of personal statements brought me to my knees.

IMPEACHED

Confession

Perhaps it is best we do not assemble
On opposing sides of my "interview station".
I would *not* have asked your motivation
For medicine, nor implied the dept. would enable
Your growth over years of instruction.

Inquiry

What I really want to know is:
What's the bounds of an Ellison family event,
Where do you draw your strengths,
What evokes your emotions,
Which collectibles do you favor,
Given freedom to write, what would you pen,
How can so much soul
Be effused from an expressive container,
Who are you now and what do you want to be?

Judgement

Elizabeth Hayes Ellison (EHE) applied to WSU through ERAS. Pentimento transfixed Dr. Singer

Ms. Ellison was invited to interview.

She thanked him for the invite (first ever to do so).

EHE conveyed in a timely fashion her inability to attend.

Summary: Ms. Ellison is absolved from further contact with WSU.

Contrition

I realize there are things
Of which you may speak, and things
Of which I will never gain knowledge.
They are yours.
You are free to travel and share
Your summer mornings
With whom you wish, without repent.
I am but humbled to have known you electronically.

FACE TIME

The cautious candidates for residency had electronically maximized their efforts to present a well-rounded, professional package. Having gained acceptance for a personal interview, the savy predicted and prepared to respond to standard questions. Further, they memorized a broad theme of questions they could raise if they were permitted a reign of inquiries.

Most candidates presented themselves in conservative dark suits, and matching behaviours meant to conform to implied expectations. Whether unstructured or structured at a given institution, the verbal exchange was typically stereotypical. It was difficult in this contrived environment to determine what truly made someone tick. When you engaged a cluster of candidates for thirty minutes each, expansion of character was unusual. You were left to judge non-verbal clues.

A dead fish handshake was deadlier than a 50th percentile standardized test score. A rigid, unchanging posture or artificial smile negated a warm letter of recommendation. Poor eye contact or sweaty brow contradicted qualifications highlighted by an advisor. A favorable depiction of character by the Dean could be canceled by excessive gestering or nervous twitches.

ANALYSIS OF OUR INTERVIEWS

Content

An introductory salutation and open hand
Precede the quest for what's critical and relevant:
"What brings you here today?" Another liberating demand,
"Tell me how you feel," is an efficacious abdicant.
Sequentially we seek, "How long have you felt this way?"
And, "What have you done to improve your condition?"
"Do family, other physicians know of what you've conveyed?"
Or, "What are your expectations from my opinion?"
The paradise of succinct response is too often lessened
By some hidden agenda or misspoken revelation.

Subjects

Due to the complexity of their past histories
We've reviewed the Dean letter pamphleteers.
Within, biographies often note contention with adversity.
Supervisors laud the sufficiency of a student's character.
Clerkship directors translate their accomplishment to grades.
The weighted average leads to a quartile caricature.
Fourth-year E.D. audition reports are written to persuade.
NBME's above 200 cast a promise on their future.
The countenances are deceptive; with garlands removed
They're not all jewels–balanced, tempered and smooth.

Interpretation

Handsomely attired, we're confident and polished
At extracting what motivates and exhilarates.
We project construction of a Match that embellishes
The Department, and beyond enriches all the Diplomates.
In this courtship we afford each sufficient attention.
They leave our offices with business cards in hand.
We ask them to write or call for lingering questions.
Escorted without instruction, they're discharged "in demand."

We'll discount dissuasory measures if we're enamored
And pardon eccentricities for scholarship that's unslumbered.

Outcome to Embrace

The energy expenditure to emulate and complete
This process, particularly when repeated without interlude
Is great, yet only hesitantly should we retreat
From a compassionate and inquisitive attitude.
Let us strive for this structured respect in the E.D.!
We need to make efforts to preserve and cultivate
Patients' identity; those in our medical trust have uncertainties
In their lives that rival those of resident candidates.
Folks will continue to appear before us journey-weary.
We may alter biographies of all, with cogent queries.

Reprinted with permission from *Academic Emergency Medicine* 3:358-359, 1996

Despite the intense emotional scrutinity and misplaced analysis we subjected upon each other during the interview process, I looked forward to meeting each candidate. No matter how artificial, I had an opportunity each year to meet a highly qualified group of my future colleagues.

My efforts were not to determine what type of lettuce they would be were they a salad. Instead, I tried to sustain them in conversation about what was central to their life. Inquiry that concentrated on free time activities typically reduced their protective guard. I could easily project working alongside an individual in the E.D. when they were willing to discuss openly and honestly the merits of their culinary habits. I envisioned the suitability of someone's match for my professional zeal by their descriptons of baseball card, butterfly or antique collection. Their intensity of illumination regarding earlier pursuits in life were also revealing.

RENAISSANCE ENDEAVORS

A majority of the residents who ultimately matched in our training program were naturally gifted science majors. They were salutorians or valadictorians in high school who academically over-achieved in college. They were members of honor societies as undergradutes and many were elected to Alpha Omega Alpha, the national honor society reserved for the top ten percent of medical students. A good percentage of our residents were also driven outside the classroom to be civic leaders, responsible to their local or regional communities, politically active and religiously responsible.

The less naturally-gifted residents were hard-working, motivated, compliant and effective college students. They too may have majored in sciences but there was a tendency toward diversity.

Those who entered the workforce as an accountant, banker, pharmacist or engineer ultimately demonstrated skills far above their peers. Somehow they developed a spark for medicine and changed direction. After they had mastered the medical school curriculum, many retained and applied their previous skills and interest.

Talent was palpable. As a few examples, Drs. Randy Marriott, Tim Manual and Jim Brown effectively escalated their premed school activities as fire fighters into emergency physicians with prehospital interests. Dr. Phil Froman, who had been a fire chief for nine years, applied his administrative skills to our benefit as one of our chief residents. Similarity, Dr. Sharon Malone during her year as a chief resident took charge with aplomb, in part from her previous tenure as owner of a self-started fashion business. Dr. Pat Panelli and Dr. Rick Lucht drew light to their presentations or writings from their formal and informal stints as a medical illustrationist and cartoonist, respectively. Dr. Kevin Kulow, who enjoyed sky diving, joined the Dayton SWAT Team. During residency he scored second in a national competition for marksmanship. He placed more bullets into a simulated hostage taker's forehead from 200 yards than any professional assassins.

Many of the residents were equally talented, but their repertoires were more subtle. Sports were the exception. Dr. Jennifer Swanson, an Olympic equestrian, was comparatively reserved, but others who had been previously drawn into organized sports reasserted juvenile behaviors at any departmental athletic event. The outcome was injury. The list of wounded over the years has been lengthy. From roughly 100 men and women who participated with abandon, the list of wounded has been lengthy. The injuries and mechanisms I recall included bruised ego—golf cart expulsion; fractured cervical spine—football; shoulder injury and loss of consciousness—football; ankle—football; fractured ribs and punctured lung—football; facial fracture—football; fractured forearm—baseball; and fractured forearm—football. Three additional doctors exacerbated preexisting knee injuries during our annual Turkey Bowl football outing and each subsequently required surgery to repair ligamentous damage.

In addition to weekend warrior activities, our residents also attempted to validate their self-perceived infallability on the imaginery field of health. Only when they developed incapacitating neurologic deficits did three separate residents undergo back, brain and neck surgery. Pneumonia ultimately confined one resident to a hospital room. He conceded defeat with greater reluctance than another resident who required admission to the I.C.U. for an asthma attack. We've had residents who insisted on continuing patient care while they themselves suffered from various ailments which included influenza, viral meningitis, gall bladder attack, excruciatingly painful passage of kidney stones and extensive second degree burn to the hand.

LEANING AIN'T UNNECESSARY WHEN YOU'RE BENT

Our function for others is to mend and heal;
From booboos on fingertips to codes -
Each grief is a matter of relativity.
We staff the floors, a unit, many ED's
Repeatedly awakened by war's alarm of illness
That sound and sever tranquility.
In or outpatient, as we go forth where danger lies,
We pray for others to remain unharmed

And sorrowfully, nary is the call to our own Godmother.
Yet, it is oft' that harm or hurt we meet
And what is our response? Suck-up, Endure!
We need no gash nor amputation from cannonball
To strike us down; not impervious, we too are mortal.
None will be annoyed with advance of your complaints:
Whatever your occupation, fail not to secure your health.

Reprinted with permission from *Academic Emergency Medicine* 1:60, 1994

INTANGIBLE REWARDS

Over their three-year experience, I was able to establish and maintain close association with a good number of residents. During the many hours together, we gratified our professional pleasures and enjoyed each other's company. I took delight in watching many residents blossom.

In his premedical school life as an atypical paramedic, Rick Hunt taught others, conducted research and published nearly a dozen papers. When we met, he was applying for a position as a resident in emergency medicine. Every aspect of his countenance smiled. When his mouth was in motion with a bashful, stuttering, eastern Carolina drawl, his eyes still twinkled. Feeling comfortable with him after only a few minutes, I suggested he could skip the residency and fill a vacant faculty position. He matched with us, learned well the wide field of emergency medicine and continued his pursuits in the prehospital care arena. Before graduation he had shown by his independent research that paramedics, if provided a Polaroid camera, could capture the car damage at a crash sight enabling the emergency physician to predict the extent of passenger injuries. In another research project he documented our inability to diagnose chest problems during helicopter evacuation from a crash scene. The rotors made too much noise. So did Rick. His vocalizations resulted in eventual promotion to Chairman, Department of Emergency Medicine at State University of New York, Syracuse.

Trace spent many years in south Florida emergency departments as a physician assistant. Over the years, he gained some independence from supervising emergency physicians, but eventually grew tired of his limitations. Frustrated, he took out his steam riding motorcycles. During his emergency medicine residency with us, he used his cerebral powers to write several papers. He abandoned fast vehicles for parenthood. Wife, Lucy, bore their first born, Zachary Dayton Weiner, before they returned to native Florida. I was proud to be present in their home when the little guy lost his foreskin.

Dr. Roger Pacholka has been our department's most faithful relief worker. During residency, he established contact within the medically underserved continent of Africa. After his graduation, he periodically returned to the villages where he provided care. Each time he brought needed medical supplies and an ever-expanding contingent of emergency medicine residents and faculty to lessen medical burdens. In his premedical school days he lessened human misery by bringing comic relief to listeners of a Dayton hard rock radio station. To my knowledge, no other irreverent disk jockeys have similarly expanded their vocal rituals to include missionary work beyond their listening borders.

I was privileged to have temporarily shared the intellectual daring and spirit with many other physicians in training. Unfortunately, I did not tell them often enough of how I celebrated their successes.

A FATHER'S DAY MESSAGE TO DRURY

Speech, ultimately a reflection of self
Or at minimum, a mirror of the soul
From Drury there's temperance and self-control.
His clinical introduction lends towering confidence
To any tobacco harvesting Kentuckian.
Behind every ya'll there's diligence, strength of will
According to any John Deer rider from hill and hollar.
Every woman with a slop pail recognizes self-control;
Each man with a dung fork in hand notes temperance.

Before this prestigious group I now plead:
Look beyond that mint juliped,
Sour mashed, hominy grit utterance
And admit as I, he's the man you'd like
To treat your aging father when he faces calamity.

THE TONIC OF AOA

The Alpha Omega Alpha medical honor society was established to recognize superior academic and scholastic accomplishment. In recent time, medical students were elected to A.O.A. who appeared to have most accurately mastered the curriculum and unlocked their talents for the benefit of the medical community. The Epsilon Chapter representing the State of Ohio permitted late acceptance of individuals, who during residency or beyond had shown extraordinary fertility.

As Program Director, I yearly recommended a third-year emergency medicine resident who was an insightful, accurate craftsman for induction to A.O.A. With a several-page note I annually sketched a narrative that characterized the candidate's generous outburst of character. Although the A.O.A. Induction Committee overlooked many residents I nominated, they accepted over the years Drs. Darin Pangalangan, Jane Uva, Brian Dursteler, Joan Kolodzik and Max Lee. They well deserved this gift of affection.

Dr. Frank Smeeks, an emergency medicine resident who had been elected to A.O.A. at Meharry College, nominated me as a W.S.U. faculty member for induction into A.O.A. Frank suggested to the Ohio Chapter that I possessed gifts beyond my own knowledge. They were not overwhelmed by his presentation. Upon receipt of my rejection, I responded in verse.

DEAR SIRS: RE ENTERING THE HALLS

I've progressed from the talented, never considered
To the "worthy of consideration," but denied.
Unlike the sport veterans whose stats are fixed

Before next year I can modify the RBI's or assists.
Pass on thanks to the Committee members who pondered.
I'm conditioned to ask "Sir can I have another?"

Despite nonsurvival of their scrutiny, the following year I was invited to present at their induction ceremony. I briefly lent voice from a podium and read the following congratulatory verse:

SUMMONED

This pendant divides an already
Distinguished community into two sects:
Those with a habit of cloistered study
And those whose book of knowledge
Or service has uplifted beyond hope.
A few aspire, stand strong in spirit
That they're clothed in A.O.A. as juniors.
Other's golden deeds do triumph in four.
On occasion, the apt award of praise
Is reserved for grads whose judgement inspires.
With your contributions to medicine
May these lofty folks of earthly letters
Welcome you with heart to a higher place.

The following year, the Chapter determined that only a Program Director who belonged to A.O.A. could nominate someone for A.O.A. I found their attempt to silence unauthorized opinion unacceptable. My pen did not lie moored in a quiet harbor.

VOCALIZATIONS FROM ONE OF THE KINSHIP

We're physicians of the human community
Tenacious of purpose for the achievement of health.
We accept unfrenzied applause of fellow citizens.
Stirred without argument for our rightful cause.

The A.O.A. Society orchestrates the honored sung,
Disposed to excellence in their critical mirror.
At equal station, inductees are free to follow charter
And constitute plus keep their self-made laws.
Let me caution the draftsmen re: perpetuating praise.
The unelected are rightful members, one of another
Who clamor to acclaim those peers who transcend.
Firmly resolved should never be exclusion barred.
Mind the family's insurgent by letting injustice end.

I think the vessel of A.O.A. fatigued from my stone-throwing at their portholes. They ultimately opened the hatch and I've stood on deck, not creating too great a list.

NAVIGATING A COURSE

At Wright State University School of Medicine I had taken a professional voyage among friendly faces, largely free of obstruction. No one imposed a barrier to ascending the academic ladder. In 1991 I became the nation's second Professor of Emergency Medicine and Pediatrics. I was thrilled to join Dr. J. Alex Haller, Jr., a passionate pediatric surgeon at Johns Hopkins University, who was the first. I think Alex enjoyed my entrance into what would become an expanding fraternity.

Dr. Haller was one of God's masterpieces. When He painted the canvas of this earth with a jauntiness that comes with long practice, The Lord created pink, soft-faced Alex. Where eyebrows and lashes were typically obliged, the area lay naked. His scalp was bare. Alex was fated to confront alopecia totalis, the absence of any body hair. If he had displayed any length of self-consciousness, it was resolved well before our first meeting. I looked forward to repeated encounters. Alex was always buoyant. A typical meeting would go something like this:

"Alex, how are you?"

"I'm fine, Jonathan. I've gotten grayer since we last saw each other; it's just not showing on my head."

Alex and I were originally drawn in 1980 to a conference table in Knoxville, Tennessee by Dr. Martha Bushore. Martha's avowed intention was to improve the nation's delivery of care to children who sought help for illness or injury in our emergency departments. She gathered a cadre of emergency physicians and surgeons. From all over the country, to my mystification, experts endowed with special talent each hugged Martha before joining in prolonged group discussion.

Although Martha disagreed with several early participants, including Alex, she sacrificed herself, repeatedly pushed on the fragile door of political harmony, and over a period of years established a prestigious body, The Advanced Pediatric Life Support (A.P.L.S.) Task Force Committee. The American Academy of Pediatrics (A.A.P.) and American College of Emergency Physicians (A.C.E.P.) financially and philosophically lent their support to the Committee's work. The committee ultimately developed a model curriculum (including textbook, slide series and workbook) for a standardized national course.

Martha invited me to Chicago to help her present the first A.P.L.S. Course. The presentation was electrifying, not because of the subject matter, but the result of being together with Martha. The fiercely-won, hot fluid of A.P.L.S. coursed through Martha's resilient flesh. I had the fortune to see and hug her numerous times, long after she polished the A.P.L.S. Course, and turned the A.P.L.S. Task Force Committee over to others.

GROWTH OF PEDIATRIC EMERGENCY MEDICINE

In 1975, while I explored the fetal development of pediatric emergency medicine in Cincinnati, Drs. Steve Ludwig and Gary Fleisher gave birth to the specialty on the East Coast. They consolidated the elements of knowledge and experience under their direction and established premier fellowships for pediatric emergency medicine in Philadelphia and Boston. In two decades of expansion that followed, over 60 other medical centers offered fellowship programs. The initial parents of these training programs and the subspecialty itself were initially A.A.P. and A.C.E.P. However, the organizations that legitimized the birth were the American Board of Pediatrics (A.B.P.) and American Board of Emergency Medicine (A.B.E.M.).

The A.B.P., housed in North Carolina and A.B.E.M., located in Michigan were formal buds on the branches of the complex organizational tree of medicine. The two bodies worked with a Chicago bud, the American College of Graduate Medical Education (A.C.G.M.E.). The A.C.G.M.E. assured an institution that offered pediatric emergency medicine fellowship training had translated the policies and procedures for training into an effective educational program. The A.B.P. and A.B.E.M. certified that a physician through completed fellowship had effectively harnessed all the information and skills offered by the institution. In order to be certified as a pediatric emergency physician, a candidate had trained in an A.C.G.M.E. accredited institution and passed a written examination coauthored by representatives of the A.B.P. and A.C.E.P.

A quarter decade after my commitment to a concept, a large number of other certified pediatric emergency medicine specialists have reinforced the wisdom of my decision. As a body, they are the second largest group of certified pediatric subspecialists. Like me, I suspect they've framed their numbered certificate of accomplishment. I know that Drs. Ludwig and Fleisher's diplomas bear 0001 and 0002. I proudly display my certificate bearing 0005 on my office wall.

CHANGE NEED NOT ALTER THE FEEL

**For the group now practicing as baby boomers
Existent choices were Old Spice and English Leather.
In retrospect, they were masculine, unfettered scents
Whose olfactory patterns inspired a confident strut.
We had Levi's and the new competitors, Wranglers.
Neither were stone washed, relaxed fit or boot cut.
In the E.D., few formal cloths were standard wear.
The sense docs strained to convey was unambiguous;
We've replaced the less equipped, trained on-the-job
Contingent whose patterns of practice we've not applied.**

Now the pheromones that attracted are less palpable.
Yes, the hems are frayed and the knees unraveled.
No sensible man ever pitched well worn, contoured denims.
None should reject a practice burdened by *anything* unpleasant.

Reprinted with permision from *Academic Emergency Medicine* 7:686, 2000

STRUGGLING WITH POWERS OF THE PEN

A.C.E.P. and A.B.P. fostered the assembly of members with common interest and purpose into "sections." I belong to the pediatric emergency medicine sections of both organizations. Over the years, the sections focused on current and future problems and needs in the emergency care of children. I gave of no more time and personal resources than others on multiple collaborative projects. However, I voluntarily committed fulfilling hours to their writing and editing projects.

Outside of task forces, committees, and section activities, I searched and experimented with various editing and writing techniques. Without concurrence of others, I can only arbitrarily claim success. Yet without underestimating my journalistic faults or overstating the impact of my pen, I am nevertheless free to celebrate my literary legacy. I have committed over 150 commentaries, articles, abstracts, poems and chapters to the medical literature as well as co-edited or edited a handful of manuals and textbooks. Unfortunately, I can not manipulate an historical editing record that was the result of my acting out.

THE IMPACT OF THROWING EGGS, RAGS, AND INSULTS

I don't recall the context of the disagreement
But know that we were sharing a brunch.
The tenor of the debate somehow escalated.
I flipped two over-easy past the hutch.
The yolks exploded on the curtains.
Distempered, I walked the block, and apologized.

My wife reaffirmed her choice of a mate.
A decade later from the central aisle
I winged a wet wash cloth high and right
Of her unsettled head to punctuate a point.
No walks; I finished the dishes and apologized.
Mrs. Singer reaffirmed the choice of her children's father.
Of late, after arduous preparation to revise
The pediatric section of an EM text
A proposition between two matched sides led
To straightforward verbiage being pointedly tossed
Across the breakfast table at a Chicago hotel.
The senior editor and I imploded.
I took a walk to the airport after delivering an apology.
Even when their actions have been provoked,
Unintentioned, or marks left only emotional,
I've never had an affinity for abusers.
Alas, eggs, rags, and insults have been my bane.

Reprinted with permission from *Academic Emergency Medicine* 5:1090, 1998

I have a sense the publishing company forgave my misconduct, but the senior editor retained her displeasure.

FORGIVENESS

From all recorded accounts, occasions were rare when Jesus did not forgive. No matter how many psychometric properties I have shared with Jesus, I've rarely forgiven. Examples are plentiful, especially in the earlier stages of my professional associations. Nothing better illustrated my perverse tendencies than disparate confrontations with Dr. Lester Sanders and Dr. Roger Barkin.

Two significantly ill children of a household were brought to the E.D. for care. Unknown to me at the father's request, the triage clerk placed a page for Dr. Sanders. I was in the process of determining the most appropriate course of action for the children when I was advised by a nurse that Dr. Sanders wished to speak with me on the phone. I reported my findings and told Dr. Sanders I would acquire blood studies and initiate intravenous therapies to the brothers. He responded in an indignant fashion, "These are my patients, and the course you'll follow is what I determine to be in their best interest." Without response, I hung up the phone and returned to the side of the children to initiate treatment. Under the pretense I was assisting with their intravenous line insertions, I refused to come to the phone for Dr. Sanders' second power attempt. I was shortly thereafter invited to explain my side of events to the Chief of Staff. He gently chastised me and advised me to write a letter of apology. The letter was my last communication with Dr. Sanders. We avoided eye contact when we crossed paths each week at the hospital's Grand Rounds. We never spoke in the remaining five years he had on this earth.

I suspect neither Dr. Barkin or I will engage in conversation before we return to dust. In 1981, he asked me to author a chapter in the first edition of his pediatric emergency medicine textbook. I missed the date for submitting my final draft by a month. When I completed the chapter I initiated a phone conversation. He indicated that he had unsuccessfully made attempts to call me when the deadline had passed. When we didn't connect, he wrote the chapter himself.

For a decade I had no further contact with Dr. Barkin. He was assigned an hour to present to emergency physicians assembled at a conference in Maui, Hawaii. I was to follow. None of the conference architects monitored the talks. They were occupied with modifications of the land created by Trent Jones. I was standing at the rear of the room by the audio visual supporter as Dr. Barkin's time should have expired. Recognizing he had at least 15 minutes more of material that would have extended into my allotted hour, I mischievously withdrew his carousel of slides, had the projectionist display my lead and walked boldly to the podium. Dr. Barkin's not-so-congratulatory view of my approach suggested he understood the unspoken nature of my lesson regarding a need for timely completion of tasks.

Unfortunately, I had similarly shared marginally merited wrath with various non-professionals. Additionally, I had bestowed unmerited wrath upon my family, especially my sister, Mickie.

Mickie was between her second and third year of life when she inoffensively invaded Pepper's space during a routine meal. Pepper ingloriously snapped at Mickie's hand. The event for this half-cocker, half-something else species was a minor outlet of frustration. Being of a comparable age of Mickie, he simply was asserting his principled right to eat from a dog bowl without Mickie's intrusion. I supported Pepper's request for space, even when he nightly challenged my own, lying cordially at my seven-year-old side in bed.

Within a few months of the original misdeed, Pepper rationally penetrated a canine into Mickie's face when she liberally yanked on his tail. Father, defending his youngest child's artistic authority, took unapproving alarm with Pepper's impudence. I was not in harmony with Pop's all too prompt decision to give Pepper to a childless couple who resided in the country. Since the evening I lost my four-legged companion, I've resented my sister.

ILLUMINATIONS FROM THE FAMILY

POKEY, OUR FIRST BORN

Mickie, brother Barry, and I brought little calm to our parents. Fully knowing that children were inherently disruptive to parental peace, I nonetheless conceded a strong desire to start a family with Ruth. She and her sister, Judy, had maintained harmony during their youth. Ruth witnessed multiple couples enrich their lives through investments in child rearing. Despite positively evaluating her own parent's experiment and seeing the joy a dozen kids brought their immediate neighbors, Ruth was hesitant to bring children into the world. She lacked confidence in her parenting skills. I was convinced the addition of a pet in our lives would facilitate Ruth's mastery of mothering. Neither Ruth nor I anticipated the baptismal warning generated by Pokey.

His mother was one-half cocker. His father was fast. Only Lil's kids, responding abruptly to a commotion, barely witnessed him rescaling a four-foot fence in retreat. He was potent. The four female pups were promptly spoken for by neighbors. Ruth was among Lil's coworkers invited to meet the three unadopted six-week-old male pups.

On a Sunday afternoon we went to look, not grope and find him. But we did. We took home the runt of the litter. Ruth accepted the name Pokey, after the lovingly miscreant animal in *The Pokey Little Puppy*, a book repeatedly read to me by my parents as a sleep tonic.

At our bedtime, Ruth and I placed Pokey in a cardboard box containing a blanket and loudly ticking clock. They served poorly to quiet his separation anxiety. By midnight, I removed him from the locked kitchen and brought him to our bedroom. His crying ceased until Monday morning when Ruth left for her 7 AM - 3 PM shift. Near my 7:30 AM departure he was shivering in hysteria. I took Pokey with me to work.

In violation of all health regulations, the consenting charge nurse at University Hospital permitted me to convert the pediatric treatment room 1 into a veterinary day care center. No one suffered ill effects of the departments reduced occupancy until 3 PM, which coincided with the nursing change. In my estimate, the second shift nurse spontaneously lost more body fluids when she uncovered my new family member than Pokey passed all day. Before my departure, which was not soon enough to suit an uptight (but correct) nurse, I sanitized counters and mopped the floor.

I cleaned errant urine and stool from many surfaces for quite some time. Pokey, long after he was seemingly potty-trained, deposited his gifts everywhere in our apartment. When we moved the following year to our house, Pokey's presents were less palatable. His misbehavior affronted Ruth but was tolerated until we purchased furnishings for an empty living room. Before the delicate legs of a love seat could indent the wool fibers of the virgin area rug, Pokey lifted his hind leg. Ruth witnessed his stream of violation and seized. Her unsettled head punctuated many points, including the ultimate threat, "It's either him or me; one of us is leaving!"

The compromise to loss of wife or offspring was enrollment into obedience school. Pokey and I feared the drill sergeant, but we weathered the Thursday evening classes. After twelve weeks Pokey passed with two grade points above the minimum, and one point above a wire terrier that was a certified psychological cripple and an embarrassment to the dog kingdom. More important than the percent number on Pokey's diploma, Ruth's brewing point lowered; the magnitude of Ruth's heat with Pokey's relapses did not escalate to threats of divorce.

My four-legged firstborn had issues. Voluntary loss of bowel and bladder control alternated with destruction of clothing, sheeting, drapes, leather goods and door frames. We slowly recognized these evils sprang from abandonment. When we were both at work or spent an evening out of the house together, a spirit moved our son to ambush the household. We poorly understood what precipitated his prolonged, uncontrolled outbursts against sirened vehicles or the ring of a doorbell. Noise was not the precipitant. On the Fourth of July he would summon no vocalization and cowered, pleading for our support. There was no rational explanation for his rage at seeing someone in uniform. Pokey wagged his tail and sought reaffirmation from Rich, our friend, when he entered our yard as a neighbor. When Rich approached via the same access route in his garbageman's uniform, Pokey charged, bared his teeth as if to suppress an invader from the dominion of Satan. For almost two full years beyond Pokey's death, we found handwritten suggestions on Fed Ex or UPS packages, warning the deliverer of a potential monster.

Pokey's sexually deviant behavior was a contributing factor to his early demise. In his first five years, he was outdoors only with direct supervision in the yard or on leash. He knew nothing of females. He satisfied his sexual frustrations by autoerotic behaviors. In the inhospitable winter of 1976, when I refused to be walked in the cold by a dog's urges, I unleashed him. He immediately became the sexual partner of Cindy, a well-mannered mutt who never left the confines of her backyard. Despite Cindy's monogamous relationship with Pokey, he indiscreetly roamed the neighborhood during a decade of liberation. He was struck at age 14, crossing the street in pursuit of sexual favors. He sustained a femur fracture and dislocated hip. His arthritic preinjured body was in a state of decline. He was preferentially immobile, unless obliged to chase a squirrel or pathologically charge against Ruth or me if we hugged one of the children at the back door on their way to school. Since I literally had to repeatedly kick Pokey in self-defense to prevent our injury the very morning of his last day, I made the decision to have him euthanized. He may have surgically recovered from his physical injuries, but he was psychologically lame.

EUTHANIZING TIGGER

I was an emotional cripple after Pokey's death. It would be a decade before a frail, less-than-a-handful-sized kitten filled my pet void. Tooney grew to become a member of the family. A few years later, we added

Tigger. She too grew, somewhat to excess such that we nicknamed her "Fatbutt."

Sadly, Tigger insidiously became ill in her third year of life. I thought I had poisoned her from mineral spirit vapors, but in true style of a C.P.C., I was shown to be a poor clinician.

FELINE CPC: "SHE'S NOT HERSELF"

Barricaded on the wrong side of a door
During a bedroom rehabilitation project
She was exposed to volatile hydrocarbon odors
With acute liver, brain, or marrow threats.
A self-imposed NPO sequentially profaned
Motor tone, speech, and an abdominal silhouette.
The last micturate was on our bed sheets–
A void dispassionately released from hindbrain.
"Look at her, she's not her usual self?"
An expression of disbelief we've all heard
Repeatedly and uniformly ignored the import
Was an echoing hidden agenda to explore.
In the department she was febrile and dry
Without focus of infection, neurologically adrift.
LFTs up, Na low, increased count with left shift;
AP bodygram revealed abnormal bowel afloat.
Unresponsive to intravenous amp and gent
They let me know her abdominal tap
Yielded polys and sheets of gram negs.
They sought permission for an exploratory lap.
A transmural tumor permitted ileocecal
Contents to soil the peritoneal cavity.
Mets were present in the regional nodes.
Mass, not mineral spirit, invaded the liver.
Tigger, full member of our family, was euthanized.
Her loss was reminiscent of my biologic kindred
Who died when I was in a double coverage mode.

At times, colleagues willfully pull our load.

Reprinted with permission from *Academic Emergency Medicine* 4:863, 1997

FAILURE AT BIRTH DOCTORING

In the early morning hours rain froze on the roadways. The four inches of snow that followed snarrled traffic. Ruth and I could get no closer than a mile to our work at the hospital. The vigorous walk may have been a contributory factor to the onset of her labor that evening.

Midway through labor at the hospital was uneventful. Then I noted Ruth's contractions were followed by a significantly reduced fetal heart rate. These late decelerations signified the fetus was distressed. I called the ominous fetal monitor recording to the attention of the obstetrician. He confidently told me the contractions were variable, suggesting no problem existed. However, he thought it advisable that I change from my street clothes into surgical scrubs *now*. They were taking Ruth to the delivery room and a C-section was likely. From the father's waiting room I called Dr. Bill Keenan, a neonatologist who I had come to admire and trust when he served as my attending physician during residency. While struggling with my clothing, I froze at the cover page title on a medical journal that had been inadvertently interspersed among lay magazines. It read, "Why is this baby not breathing?"

Bill Keenan arrived in time to see Matt's first futile breath. Ruth asked why she heard no cry. What was audible, a struggled grunt, suggested a problem with the heart or lungs. Bill delivered oxygen to Matt's face and hustled him to the N.I.C.U. I told Ruth I was hungry for a hamburger and without further explanation abandoned her before hearing a disappointing reply. With Bill's help we stabilized Matt and he recovered within hours from the tightly wound umbilical cord that had depleted the oxygen to his vital organs.

I thought I had recovered completely, yet eighteen months later I nervously summoned Bill Keenan again. The obstetrician all but buried his forearm up to the elbow in Ruth's pelvis trying to rotate Pete into a position that would permit his delivery. When the obstetrician's grip was insufficient, he clamped a two-foot-long stainless steel prong to both sides of Pete's head and face. Like a rodeo contest, he applied a rotational force that would have brought a steer to the mud rink floor. Pete refused to turn. Bill arrived to watch Pete be forcep extracted, face up, 180^0 from a normal descent. Bill confirmed Pete's good health and restored my calm.

I carelessly brought home influenza from the hospital and infected the boys and Ruth. While in the height of her illness, Ruth experienced headache, fever, cough and total body aches that were worse than labor pains. Hours into frequent contractions, with a hoarse voice, Ruth pitifully lamented her stalled progress. Then her water broke, revealing dark green fluid. Liz, stressed in utero, had defecated and was at risk of inhaling the thickened fluid into her lungs. Bill responded to my panicked call. The scrub nurse obliged my request to open the neonatal resuscitation packet. I hooked up the suction device, checked the light source on the intubation equipment and set out three sizes of endotracheal tubes. I was prepared to prevent a life-threatening event called meconium aspiration. Ruth had several titanic contractions. I engaged the onsite OB resident. My pleading succeeded to help him deliver Liz. Bill arrived like the calvary for the third time. He suctioned Liz's air passage and permitted my normal breath.

In the recovery area, I told Ruth, "I love you, but you do a lousy job of delivering babies." Since she finally had her little girl, she told me she intended to have no further obstetrical adventures. I had reversed her denial three times previously and had an outside chance for a fourth. However, Bill shortly thereafter left to head a neonatal program in St. Louis. A birth without Dr. Bill Keenan's proximity would be too unnatural!

WHEN BEING A PHYSICIAN HELPED

One evening at six months of age, Matt refused to sleep. I convinced Ruth to not approach his crib. Only when she grew intolerant, I opened the nursery door to find him febrile and ill-appearing. By my exam his lingering cold had progressed to ear infection. I had just documented a paternal error in permitting Matt to suffer alone in his room. Ruth distrusted my instinctual plan to initiate antibiotic treatment for his ear infection. She demanded an opinion of a "real doctor."

Matt and I made it through the system at the E.D. by 2 AM. The physician on duty suggested the eardrum changes I observed were the result of prolonged crying. We were sent home without antibiotic treatment. Upon arising, I discovered pus had rolled out the left ear onto Matt's sheet. The infection had perforated his ear drum.

Years later Pete displayed a fever, high-pitched, barking cough and difficulty breathing consistent with a severe case of croup. On the second evening of his illness, I watched his ribs retract with every breath. He needed a breathing treatment with a drug called racemic epinephrine. At the time of his illness, the medication was given by inhalation to those patients who were admitted to the hospital. From home at approximately midnight I contacted Dr. Ed Lowe, the on-call pediatric anesthesiologist at the hospital, who granted outpatient treatment for Pete. After Pete's relieving treatment, I reclined between two of my office chairs and Pete slept until daylight on my chest.

At birth, Liz's right lower leg turned the right foot inward and the left lower leg turned the left foot outward. This rotational problem, called a windswept deformity, corrects itself after a child begins to walk. Dr. Devoe twice encouraged Ruth to take Liz to an orthopedist. My objection was ultimately overruled. Grandma Hoenemeyer accompanied Ruth at Dr. Aaron Pearlman's and witnessed his application of plaster casting from Liz's knees to her toes. Before Liz's second casts were removed four weeks later, I encountered Aaron in the doctors' lounge.

"Jon," he said, "the deformity would correct itself, but I knew with serial castings I could straighten Liz's legs out easily."

In only a partial truthful response, I replied, "Thanks, Aaron, I appreciate your care."

Despite my in-laws' and wife's lingering reservations, I tended to the children's injuries, including suturing their lacerations and treated their infectious diseases with antibiotics when I felt they were indicated.

In their collective childhoods, I was a rock-stable, clinically-competent, humanistically-oriented, father-healer. Only Matt half-heartedly accused me of malpractice, when I forced him to shovel snow from the driveway two weeks after he had fallen on an outstretched arm. The x-ray we ultimately acquired the following day showed an incompletely healing fracture.

NOT FREE OF ERROR

At 17 months of age we transferred Matt from his crib to a regular bed abutting the wall. We placed a guard rail on the open side and an extra mattress on the floor to cushion a potential fall. There was a month from the time of his displacement to Pete's occupancy of Matt's former bed. Therefore, I don't think jealousy contributed to Matt's decision to wander repeatedly at about 11 PM from his new bedroom to ours. One evening he stood for 60 minutes in the corner of our room, facing the wall over the alternative choice I gave of returning to his bed. Another night in frustration I lassoed his ankle with my pants belt and knotted the other end on a bed post. Ultimately, I resorted to an inverted port-a-crib placed in the center of his room. He found comfort with the mattress on the floor and nightly asked for his "cage" as he prepared for bed.

I have lovingly referred to Matt as "our good child." Liz, at one Christmas gathering where all three returned from their separate adult worlds, pointed out her oldest brother was far from perfect. She reminded us that Ruth and I alternated appearances at traffic courts with Matt during his late adolescence. Ruth provided him morale and support when a judge reprimanded Matt for the no-fault accident that totaled our car. I was present when another judge suspended his license for exceeding the speed limit by 20 miles per hour. I elected to make the 3 AM trip to the police department in Greenhills Township when Matt was 17-years-old. I had to extract him from a two-hour jailing for curfew violation, possession and consumption of alcoholic beverages. Neither Ruth or I were present for his next accident.

ACKNOWLEDGED BENEFICIARIES OF THE GRAVEYARD SKILLED

Five hours from contact by ground transport
And a time zone difference separated us
From the unknown voice who fractured serenity.
The universal parental fear had come true;
"He was involved in a bad automobile accident."
The tragically drunken reveler on Friday night
Of a benevoloent Labor Day weekend
Entered an exit ramp of Lakeshore Drive
Spun innocent navigators in front of our son
Then pancaked his Jetta in historical record.
EMS extracted and safely packaged co-victims
In customary ways then transported multiply injured.
Northwestern Memorial ED was to secure and mend
In detachment, the pledge of our inheritance.
It was hours before we could herald tomorrows.
From Allison's cell phone, Matt's c-spine protected
Voice sent emotional blazes through our darkness!
"Pops, I'm OK, they're intubating the gunshot wound."
Our prayers were answered in that exchange.
We thank more than our Heavenly Father
For emergency professionals with healing powers.

Reprinted with permission from *Academic Emergency Medicine* 9:129, 2002

As a classic, befuddled middle child, Pete was guilty of as many infractions but he was never caught. I knew what he was up to moment by moment. Since his actions at every age so much resembled mine, I felt I knew what his thoughts were before he could finalize his opinion. Our differences were slight. I don't recall sleepwalking and I don't think I ever urinated unwillfully in cupboards or trash cans. All my errant streams were conscious statements against authority.

We're unsure who transmitted Liz's windswept deformity. Without doubt, Ruth was genetically responsible for Liz's hammer toe deformities. Less visibly, but equally as clear, I passed on my learning disabilities to our daughter. From as early as her elementary school days, it was apparent Liz could not understand verbal instructions. Whenever she was read instructions for standard psychometric testing, test results suggested she was mentally retarded.

A PRODUCT OF DO AND DON'T

You are a collection of do, don't
Did, can't, want's, haves, don't know;
The perfect blend of funny bone,
Brimstone, cyclone, sinew and ozone.

Do and Don't

You're open to suggestion from coaches
But steadfast and sculpturesque in denial
Of any advice from us, your folks
Who've cajoled from infant thru juvenile.

Did and Can'ts

You became licensed despite curb waves,
Filled your tank with gas, drove a stick.
Why can't you put your laundry away,
Make change or calculate a tip?

Wants and Haves

Won't clean your room, or wash a dish
Nor go for goal in want of regalia.
Been known to throw up a few bricks,
Show dynamite "D" and lead by example.

Don't Knows

Don't know how you learned barrel stands,

To comprehend, budget time and honor roll.
Don't know that you've ever shared plans
Beyond college soccer, other long term goals.

Perfect Blend
This mythical Lizard is our minotaur
Who's invented Calabama and cactapusses,
Microwaved grilled cheese, yet digested *Octopus*.
May she always remain our loving meteor.
For all these reasons, and more, I love you.

LACKING CRITICAL SENSE

As a teacher, I attempted to help all the kids with their studies. I obviously enjoyed the opportunity to teach medical students and residents in training. I also enjoyed participating in continuing education for practicing physicians who legitimately refreshed their knowledge by attending courses. If asked by a conference organizer far enough in advance to arrange my calendar, I never refused an opportunity to speak. When a course coincided with a period of time where one or more kids could accompany me, they became part of the audience.

Liz was attentive as I delivered Grand Rounds to the Emergency Medicine Program at Methodist Hospital in Indianapolis. She enjoyed the Indiana Pacers game the night before and the museum after the two-hour talk. Both she and Pete reveled in post-conference sun at Hilton Head, South Carolina. But they reminded often that the good son was the only one invited to co-attend one of my conferences in Hawaii.

I took all three kids and Ruth to Orlando, Florida. From the airport we traveled by commercial van to the front door of the Contemporary Hotel in Disney World. The family was ten feet to my rear when the registration clerk advised me we were not registered at their facility. I produced a conference brochure from my briefcase. She reviewed the housing section and was of immediate assistance.

"Oh sir, your accommodations are at a hotel approximately one mile from the park entrance."

"How do you get there from here, if you have no means of transportation?"

She hesitated briefly and announced the solution, highlighted by a pointed finger. "Enter that gate, get on the train, exit at the parking lot and take the appropriate hotel bus."

I asked, "Do you see over my shoulder the woman and three children gathered about a pile of luggage?"

"Yes."

"They are going to kill me!"

"Oh, I'm so sorry!"

So was I. The family unequivocally recognized my mismanagement when we were temporarily denied entry beyond the turnstile without passes for the theme park. The ticket-taker yielded to my persuasion. He rapidly concluded no one would have tactfully preplanned such an illicit invasion of a fantasy land. Without supervisory opinion, he thankfully violated employee guidelines and accepted our passage. The passengers of our monorail car were less novel. They stared in slack-jawed disbelief at the first (and probably the last) family that carried suitcases in to broaden their relationship with Goofy.

INEPT TRANSFERENCE

As a family man, I tried to broaden my relationship with the community. As a physician, my friends, neighbors and city fathers automatically concluded I possessed discipline, intelligence and judgement. As a physician, I harbored the false expectation that my professional attempts at perfection would carry over into non-medical realms. There's no doubt I appreciated the gracious affection and implicit trust of non-medical colleagues, but there is equal certainty that both of our premises were periodically unjustified.

I was a partially effective assistant baseball coach. I demonstrably lost my temper only twice. The first event was near traumatic. Our power hitter punched a drive over the center fielder's reach. As my player rounded second, I picked up the discarded bat. An adolescent home plate umpire called my player out even though his spikes swipped home plate before the catcher applied the tag. In disbelief at the umpire's error, I threw the bat with unexpected force against the backstop, very nearly striking my own child in the head. I felt less foolish in the same year when I was thrown out of a ball park for persistently arguing another bad call. I told the adult ump who missed the play, "He sucked." The ump invited me to leave the park. On my way to the parking lot I deviated to tell the adult second base ump he too was a useless human being. The venting harmed no one and minimally delayed America's pastime.

On the other hand, during a high school basketball regional playoff game, Liz dribbled the ball up the court in the waning moments of a tied game, and my actions delayed the outcome of the contest for an embarrassingly long time. During the second half, the heat rose to my seat in the upper reaches of the visitors' stands. I removed my sweater. The sweater rested on my lap until the moment Liz was double teamed and knocked out of bounds. The foul, clear to all, was not called, and the ref turned the ball over to our opponent. Unexpectedly, my wadded lap apparel traveled a significant distance to mid-court, landing at the foot of a "homer" official. He was quite offended that someone's throwing arm had greater authority than their brain. Mack, our high school volunteer video photographer, had unexpectedly recorded the entire event. To my surprise, he stepped forward during a point of significant confusion and claimed that he had been the perpetrator. An arm guard escorted Mack and my sweater out of the building.

"Nazi" *(my nickname)* Bob, the supervisor of all volunteers at the A.T.P. Tennis Tournament, wanted to dismiss me, but I was the irreplaceable organizer for three consecutive years for the parents and children who consented for six days to help run one of three parking concessions. I daily presented Bob with our roster and fully understood our school's obligation to meet his staffing requirements. However, the total amount of monies raised for our school's athletic association by volunteerism reimbursed each of us at a rate of $2 per hour. I made efforts to increase the kids' enjoyment. However, I got caught illicitly shuttling a constant stream of ever-changing volunteers into a forbidden recess of the tennis stadium in order to permit them to view a portion of a center court match.

My substandard performance as a board member of a savings and loan association had greater potential to rock my community's financial status. I spent two hours every month dressed in business attire, reviewing statements of financial positioning. When I assumed my seat around the conference table, the savings and loan maintained a modest nine-million dollar portfolio of residential properties. A decade later, we boasted 45 million in assets and had expanded into commercial markets. We purchased property for one million dollars in a rapidly-expanding suburb. We tore down the property's existing family-owned motel. Within six months we came close to netting 10% in profit to a Boston-based construction firm. The sale was contingent upon financing, which unfortunately dried up for the company. Our savings and loan floundered, holding for two years one million dollars in a non-earning investment.

The federal government tightened controls on savings and loans that had begun to fail. The oversite agency phased in three higher-minimum ratios to reduce the likelihood for a governmental bailout from the Federal Deposit Incorporation Company's reserves. Concurrently, the economy soured. Commercial property and home owners fell behind on mortgage payments. We were forced to foreclose on the few who were hopelessly defaulted. We found no buyers. Our marketable assets to reserves ratio dropped. The three larger savings and loans who were in the process of negotiating our buyout suspended their interest. The government literally forced a merger of our savings and loan with a rival. Investors saw the pre-merger $10 per share stock reduced to no value. Only stock holders lost money. I lost the unforgettable sum of $52,500, but Ruth forgave my misplaced fiduciary responsibilities.

Ruth was happier to see me spend two hours every month dressed in blue jeans helping out with some household chore. I felt I was insufficiently praised for my range of acumen. As an example, she had nothing positive to say when I left remnant streaks on 52 of 52 windows I spring-cleaned in less than my allotted time. On this task and others,

I may have benefitted from direction, but I recall asking for advice on only one occasion. She was hospitalized, and I struggled with two weeks worth of childhood/adult laundering and ironing. I couldn't figure out how to effectively press the shoulders. I interrupted her post-operative course of recovery by a phone consult. By day's end I was more fatigued than anyone committed to a hospital bed. As I retired that evening, a five-line apparition appeared.

ON INTIMACY

Conjugal rights
For the evening
Of laundry day
Are justifiably
Denied.

One afternoon when we were both in physical health, Ruth offered an unsolicited critique of my bedroom vacuum cleaning. She had previously been affronted by my rudimentary knowledge base with all the machine's attachments and my tendency toward superficial efficiency. Seeing my initial strokes in the incorrect corner of the room, she projected remnant dust bunnies and commented unfavorably on my approach. I challenged the scientific validity of her analysis.

ACCEPTING RECOMMENDATION OVER SCIENCE

Those who retrieve data, analyze and offer reviews
Suggest intuition is increasingly difficult to defend.
We're exorted by these evidence canons to eschew
Decision based on experience or what "experts" contend.
I' ve learned the credible skill to refute or support;
I'm able to integrate several targeted annotations
Into my spectrum of practice and guidance of consorts.
But beware, well searched strategies have their limitations!
When advised by my spouse to start the vacuum machine

In the far corner of the bedroom, not the near
I asked, "How would my method fail to clean?"
"Common sense, practiced routine suggests you're a mutineer."
To which I replied, "Hippocrates inferred that Science
Was father of knowledge and Opinion bred no high tide."
Bringing the "office art" home can lead to abstinence.
Evidenced-based issues may be hazardous at some bedsides.

Reprinted with persmission from *Academic Emergency Medicine* 7:943, 2000

The loss of consortium was temporary.

WHERE LOSS WAS PERMANENT

Harold Solomon, friend from high school, organic chemistry study group companion for college and anatomy partner for medical school, encountered marital discord. Within a year of the birth of his twins, he lost his wife's companionship. Harold's uncertainty overtook his judgement. He lost his own life.

Chip Meyer, a small-statured but immensely strong friend in high school, grew to a man of abilities in medical school. As a family practitioner, he was held in affection by his patients. The shadows of my late afternoon lengthened precipitously when I learned of his sudden death from a heart attack.

Sadly, that was not the last time I bowed my head for medical school colleagues whose animation ceased before our expectations. Stuart Cutler, who took my official wedding pictures and with whom I journeyed on his honeymoon, died from pneumonia.

Two days before Tommy Kreindler died, I cut the portions of his hospital tray meal. The bowel cancer he silently developed seeded his liver before his jaundice announced the problem. Despite chemotherapy, the tumor thirsted for every of his body organs. The untethered masses invaded his nervous system and in piecemeal fashion destroyed his body functions.

When these friends left the womb of our medical school, no one assured a shroud would not be prematurely cast over their countenances. No guarantees were given to Brandy when she left the womb of Ruth's old roommate, Kathy. No one projected Brandy's heart would prove to be wanting. Brandy was one of the most beautiful infants I had seen. I maintain a mixture of appreciation for being present when Brandy surrendered her last breath in Kathy's arms. The loss was as agonizing as any death I had encountered, but for the first time I sensed a spirit separate from a body.

IN THE ARMS OF THE LORD

I accept the counter arguing premises how we take leave is determined by a finite governor and self impacted.

My father died because he willed it so. He tired of the slow decline of his physical and mental powers during his seventh decade. For up to 81 years, Pop had hungered for life. Breath and his family were among his most precious prizes. But a bout with influenza disrupted his fragile diabetic control, and he unemotionally announced that it was time for him to meet his maker. While Mom fiercely protected his autonomous decision, the family said their good-byes. Pop was unresponsive the following morning when I gave him a kiss before going to work. He died before my shift in the E.D. ended.

Following the loss of her soulmate, Mom's health declined. She legally certified her request for a "no code" status and asked that I prevent unhealthy toil by any of the nursing home workers in the event of a change in her consciousness.

JEAN, THIRD SHIFT "NO CODE" FROM A NURSING HOME

Despite the years, her mind retained
The memories shared by every grandmother.
Her body long ago retired,
I think sometime after the silent MI.

**She had already outlasted Dad by 18 months.
The ravages of hypertension dulled her senses
Only when diastolics exceeded 120 mmHg.
The retinopathy had partially responded to lasers.
The claudication that merely slowed her pace
Was a plus since the neuropathic gait
If brisk, led to repeated falls.
The summation invited her last year
To become a resident at "The Home."
Now, in retrospect, the chief complaint
Was only "inability to sleep."
But the Home's night nurse interpreted
A fitful state as alarming.
She phoned me; chest pain
Was a concern, EMS was sought.
As I rapidly clothed, I wondered
How a residential celebration
Of Memorial Day had been a precipitant?
2:16 a.m. and the waiting room
Was littered from an earlier rush.
Two street women in too tight shorts
Returned from a smoke break.
I was only solicited for a quarter.
Along the wall, a fatigued woman my age
Sought support from her escort's shoulder.
One of the friends of emergency medicine was at triage.
He had a headache three days ago and
Produced wrinkled, multi-colored discharge documents
From his pockets to explain his past.
His kinetics flashed "mental health!"
At 2:22, the squad arrived; lights, but no siren.
"She changed just around the corner"
They had no idea I wasn't an aid.
They thought it odd I kissed
The forehead of an uncontrollably slumped**

**Old woman who was diaphoretic and cyanotic.
Perhaps I seemed rather protective as we slipped
Through automatic doors into the empty bin of bed one.
Poor air entry, prolonged expiratory phase,
Maximal retractions, and a rate
That translated to four breaths/minute.
This was agonal for me as well.
Mom had no intentions of artificially prolonged life.
She had executed a living will.
I was in possession of this document
And a signed durable power of attorney.
Both papers were in my desk but I could
Produce neither if challenged.
"Dick come now," Glenna uttered
With an appropriate sense of urgency.
Oxygen via non rebreather was affixed.
My hand went out to Dick; he trained
At my institution a decade before.
"I don't mean to interfere, but Mom's a "no code."
The gas, and EKG, and portable chest were their reflexes.
The responses beyond were companionship,
Trust, understanding, and support.
Glenna caught my bowed head in prayer
And asked if she could make some calls,
Or would I be comforted by the clergy.
Sinus bradycardia of 44 was a prelude
To the anticipated end.
For reasons I don't understand, she converted
To sinus tach and spontaneously ventilated.
Out of the unit a week later
And informed of what had transpired
A more weakened woman inquired
"Why... I'll have to go through this again?"**

Reprinted with permission from *Academic Emergency Medicine* 2:815-816, 1995

The near-death experience was a result of a stroke. She lost a moderate amount of her right-sided strength. Her speech was unaffected, but she was selectively unable to understand the written word. With persistent effort and the guidance of therapists at the nursing home, she regained the requisite activities for daily living. Eventually, she lost the spark to live. Approximately two years after Pop's death, Mom indignantly refused to tolerate any longer the side-effects of her escalating doses of antihypertensive medications. She willed a second and fatal stroke as a peaceful end to her existence.

After a death with dignity, I discovered among her belongings a poignant narrative that follows:

"Betrayal—that's what my body does. I lie awake in my bed, listening to music, and I dance. God, how I dance! But then I consider my lack of physical strength and I devise a simple dance routine, that should express my emotions, the rhythms that surround me, and my urges to express them. And so I get up from the bed and as soon as I lift one foot a half inch from the floor, I stagger! Defeated again!

"When something drops I automatically reach down to pick it up. But only with extreme luck do I avoid falling on my face. So I lecture myself—'Stupid. Stop trying to bend down—squat instead.' Squat I do. And there I stay, unable to get up. By letting myself down on my hands and knees and crawling to the nearest chair, table or any solid object and grasping its solidity firmly, am I able to pull myself to my feet, with a great deal of effort and pain.

"What happened to that young, thin, lithe, graceful creature who still exists within this reluctant body? It can't have disappeared so rapidly. That slobby, fat, frumpy, wrinkled vision in the mirror must be somebody's idea of a practical joke. I certainly am not ready for this.

"But maybe it would make more sense if I was totally bedridden...then I'd have an excuse for my ineptitudes. What can I comfort myself with now? Old age? Of course it's old age, but old age has nothing to do with my thoughts on life. I am not ready for this yet. I bitterly resent this intrusion on my lifestyle.

"Yes, I know that this and lots more of this is to be part of my life. But I don't have to acknowledge or like it, do I? If I don't continue to fight this monster polluting me, I will have given up completely and nothing will matter anymore."

LOOKING BACK AND FORWARD

It has been said that none of us have the power to alter memory from desire. Looking back from the present doorway of my mind's dispensary, there is much that I wish had been different. Since I cannot curb nor confine the past, I look forward to altering the future. Of all wishes, I hope to learn the art of forgiveness.

BREAKPOINT FOR FORGIVENSS

Revised dictations and cautiously edited progress notes
Altering the truth would be needed to reliably decree
All our E.D. brothers and sisters to be guilt free.
Many unclothed of self-credited lies we'd facilely demote.
Why do we each define the boundaries of our acceptance?
How can one justify a toiler distracted by family tie,
Or fatigued from illogic shift forward or infirmity,
And residents moonlighting for monetary reward
Then shun the alcohol or drug addicted provider?
All these compatriots are impaired and jeopardous.
Let our maker determine the specificity for misdeed.
I'll accept uncontrolled field testing of the Almighty
Less the transgressors who fail to remain current;
The unread should be prematurely accepted into eternity.

Reprinted with permission from *Academic Emergency Medicine* 8:949, 2001

THE END

Under the guise of rationality, with this manuscript I outlined in prose and poetry selected encounters that had altered my life's navigation. The expressed stories were once a current sum of my past.

It is my hope to add to the experiences, as long as I breathe during this pilgrimage.

THE HOLY SEA

Metric flow through given vessels
Defines our demise less exacting
Than a permanent loss of conscious stream.

If given a choice, I'd prefer that impermanence of conscious thought and cessation of breath coincide. I'd hope at that point to be presented by my parents. At the posthumous ceremony they'll appear as the handsome souls on the covers of this book. May they not forfeit their stature should they introduce me as "My sum, 'the doctor'."

Printed in the United States
69513LVS00005B/121-204

9 781591 296485